X Rated Nun

X Rated Nun

◆

Woman of Integrity

Sister Jane Kelly PBVM

iUniverse, Inc.
New York Lincoln Shanghai

X Rated Nun
Woman of Integrity

Copyright © 2006 by Jane D. Kelly

All rights reserved. No part of this book may be used or reproduced by any means, graphic, electronic, or mechanical, including photocopying, recording, taping or by any information storage retrieval system without the written permission of the publisher except in the case of brief quotations embodied in critical articles and reviews.

iUniverse books may be ordered through booksellers or by contacting:

iUniverse
2021 Pine Lake Road, Suite 100
Lincoln, NE 68512
www.iuniverse.com
1-800-Authors (1-800-288-4677)

ISBN-13: 978-0-595-40984-6 (pbk)
ISBN-13: 978-0-595-85338-0 (ebk)
ISBN-10: 0-595-40984-9 (pbk)
ISBN-10: 0-595-85338-2 (ebk)

Printed in the United States of America

Contents

Part I

CHAPTER 1	My Family Background	3
CHAPTER 2	The Twins Are Born	9
CHAPTER 3	San Francisco Bound	15

Part II

CHAPTER 4	Preparing to Enter the Convent	25
CHAPTER 5	My Postulent Days	28
CHAPTER 6	My Days as a Novice	33
CHAPTER 7	My Junior Years	37
CHAPTER 8	My Final Professed Years	42
CHAPTER 9	My Years as a Superior	46
CHAPTER 10	Mistress of Junior Sisters	57

Part III

CHAPTER 11	My Years in Ukiah and Ministry to Native Americans	75
CHAPTER 12	Director of Religious Education and Planning Commissioner	81
CHAPTER 13	Plowshares	86

| Chapter 14 | Catholic Nun Blows the Whistle | 93 |
| Chapter 15 | Going Public | 96 |

Part IV

Chapter 16	My Waterloo	101
Chapter 17	I Flew Over the Cuckoo's Nest	105
Chapter 18	Departure	112
Epilogue		117

Acknowledgments

From the inception to the completion of my book, countless people have lent their skills and support

Thanks to my editor, Sarah Garguilo, who always promptly returned my phone calls and e-mails. She did a wonderful job of editing my manuscript. I maintain that an author is only as good as her editor.

I'm indebted to Jan Allegretti, who edited my first book and put me in touch with Sarah.

To my twin sister, Kay Barrow, who filled in the gaps for me and who took the time to send me photos of the family.

To Jim Barrow, my brother-in-law, who is my best critic.

To R.S. Gardner, M.D., for encouraging me to write my autobiography.

To my family members, who shared their stories with me.

To Shannon and George Phelan, for their friendship and support.

To the Sisters of the Presentation, who gave me a marvelous education and 58 years of community.

To my Covenant Community, Sisters Mary Jane Floyd, Kathleen Healy, Lucia Lodolo, Cita Herold, Maryann Healy, Marilyn Medau, Ramona Michaels and Katie Burke, who continue to include me in their group and are a source of support.

To Debra and Martin Bradley, who launched me into a whole new ministry when they invited me to open a Community Dining Room for the poor and the homeless.

To the staff at Plowshares, Mary Buckley, Rhonda De Los Santos, Beverley Metcalf, Roy Franke, Kerrie Richarson and Pilar Moreno, who go out of their way to welcome the guests and see that the daily operation moves smoothly.

To Plowshares Board of Directors, Larry MacLeitch, Ann Kilkenny, Jack Daniels, Lisa Badenfort, Will Barker, Martin Bradley, Michael Celentano, Jolinda Clark, Robert Klayman, Henrietta Munoz, Elizabeth Stephens and Norm Vroman who dedicate their time and talents to keep Plowshares an efficient organization.

To Dan and Carrie Hamburg who are dear friends and afford me so much support. Dan makes sure that I always have fire wood.

To mention everyone who came forward and supported my decision to leave the convent would take pages.

PART I

1

My Family Background

I'm convinced that what we become and what we are is largely due to who are parents were. I know that this is so true in my case.

My mother, Dorothy Doyle, came from a prominent and well-to-do family. Her father, Thomas Doyle, was a lawyer who was appointed a judge to the court of Lincoln Nebraska. His picture still hangs in the State Capitol Building. My grandfather was a devout Catholic who made sure that all of his children attended Catholic schools. Thankfully, he had the means to send them out of state to attend a Catholic High School and later a Catholic University.

Mother was an exception, since she was the youngest of six children and her father loved her dearly. He wanted to keep her close to home. It could be said that she was the "apple of his eye." She was also frail in health, prone to high blood pressure and suffered a birth defect which resulted in one leg shorter than the other and caused a hip problem that would plague her for the rest of her life. Throughout my life, I made frequent trips to the hospital to visit her. I remember on one occasion when we got to Highland Hospital in Oakland, my brother and I were so upset that our dad had to stop the car to let us out because we were both sick to our stomachs. These early experiences have left me with a dread of hospitals to this day.

On five separate occasions we witnessed my mother receiving the last sacraments. My sister Kay and I were given a high grade in our religion class because when the Sister asked if anyone in the class knew what to do if a member of the family was to be given the last rites, we were the first to raise our hands. First, you meet the priest at the door with a lighted candle and a small bell. You lead the priest to the bedside and ring the bell as you go to alert all that the priest present. Second, you have a table with cotton balls, a slice of lemon and a bowl of water so the pries can remove the holy oil from his fingers. You then leave the room so that Father can hear the confession of the sick person. When it is time to give Holy Communion to the patient, you gather at the bedside and pray. Upon hearing our explanation, the Sister was astounded at our knowledge. Unfortunately, we had plenty of practice!

I don't remember my mother's father. He only visited us once when we lived in Oakland and I have no memory of the visit. On the other hand, I knew my Grandmother Elizabeth Doyle well and can recall the many times she visited us. We always looked forward to her visits because she would always have a party and invite all of our friends. She delighted in serving the goodies herself and by the end of the party, she knew the names of all the children.

She, like my grandfather, was a native of Nebraska. Unlike my grandfather, however, she was not raised a Catholic, but converted when they were married.

Grandmother was quite a colorful lady! We have a great picture of her dressed in patriotic colors, marching down the street while holding a banner calling for women's suffrage. On another occasion, she went to the White House and asked the president to grant permission for her son, Thomas, to enroll at Annapolis. Both senate appointments were filled for Nebraska, but she was most persuasive and my Uncle "T" was admitted to the Navel Academy that year.

She was never intimidated by anyone, be it a president or a member of Congress. My mother would tell us stories of grandmother's involvement in politics. If there was an issue that grandmother felt a Congressman should address, she would call, make an appointment and take off for the State Capitol to meet with the Congressman. I can picture the Congressman, seated in a swivel chair behind his massive desk when the receptionist would announce that Mrs. Doyle was here to see him. I'm sure he said to himself, "What does the woman want now?"

I am certain that I learned from all of these stories of my grandmother that you must go to the source if you hope to bring about a change. All of my grandmother's children inherited this same passion for politics from her. My mother and Aunt Betty kept themselves well informed of candidates and propositions during election year and the Sisters at the local convent would ask them to come and explain the propositions as well as the strengths and weaknesses of the candidates. Taking after my mother, I was often asked to do the same.

My Uncle "T and Aunt Jane were frequent guests at the White House when Franklin Delanor Roosevelt was president. During the onset of World War II, as a naval officer, Uncle "T: would advise the president regarding the situation off the coast of Japan and the South Pacific Islands. Uncle "T" was commissioned as a Commodore, but would have been appointed Admiral had there been an opening.

Politics wasn't my grandmother's only passion. She was also an avid fan of the University of Nebraska football team, and legend has it that when she was seated in her reserved box the players would wave to her in recognition. She never missed a home game. When Nebraska was headed to the Rose Bowl, the team came to her house, placed a ladder leading to the second floor window, and carried her down to attend the pre-game rally!

When I was in fifth grade, my mother, my sister Kay and I traveled to Lincoln, Nebraska to spend a month visiting the Doyle's. My dad and my brother, Casey, did not go with us because dad had to work and casey didn't want to give up his magaxine route or miss that much school. Prior to our leaving, my mother had Kay and I receive our first permanent. I was terrified when they hooked us up to the machine, and rolled our hair around steel curlers. I was sure that when they removed the curlers all of my hari would go with them.

I'll never forget the excitement of seeing the huge locomotive pull in to the station with the whistle blowing, steam pouring out of the engine and the hiss of the wheels as the train braked. After boarding the train, we proceeded down the asile looking for our compartment while the train began to move and we wer challenged to keep our balance. The porter could not have done more for us. He would come and play games with us, using sugar cubes as dice. I can still picture the bowl of mints, which I can still picture—white with a mint jelly in the center. Kay and I ate so many of them that when it came time to go to diner, Kay complained that she didn't fell well. I told mother that I was fine and would go with her, but we had barely taken our seats in the dinning car when I knew that I was sick too. The rest of the trip went smoothly after that, minus the mints. We arrived in Lincoln and met our Doyle cousins, and Uncle Lum and Aunt Fitzi for the first time.

It was while we were in Lincoln that I came to know my grandmother the most. Every morning she would go to daily Mass and when she came home she would go out to the sun porch, settle in her rocking chair, light up a cigarette and read the prayers from her prayer book. We were told not to bother her while she prayed. My mother, like her mother, always went to daily Mass. It was a practice that I inherited and I rarely missed a day, right up to the time I entered the convent.

While we were in Lincoln, we stayed with Uncle Lum and Aunt Fitzi because we had to go to school. It was quite an experience. We attended St. Teresa's elementary school, the school my mother attended as a child. Siter Peter, who taught my mother, was still on the staff, though retired. The school was staffed by the Blessed Virgin Mary Order, who would arrive at school in a taxi cab because the parish was too poor to support a convent. For the first time, I learned that there was a wrong and right side of the tracks, separating the poor working class from the wealthy. There was no socializing across the tracks. This was brought home to me when I attended a birthday party and none of the children in our class were invited. They lived on the wrong side.

I missed my mother terribly during this time, and longed for the weekend when we would join her at Grandmother and Aunt Kay's house. One Saturday evening, mother and Aunt Kay were going to a party and I'll never lose the image of my mother coming down the stairs dressed in a long formal dress with a necklace of pearls and earrings to match. She was beautiful. When I hugged her, I could smell the intoxicating scent of her perfume. It would be years later that I realized the world of wealth that my mother grew up in and the contrast to the world she moved into when she and my father traveled to California.

I experienced this lavish lifestyle while staying at my Aunt Fitzi's. They had a maid, cook, and housekeeper. My cousins David and Mary were something else. Mary never walked into a room—she did cartwheels! Rarely did you see her in an upright position. She later went on to acting school and appeared in Broadway shows, eventually running a coaching school for actors in New York. David was a hellion! He tried the patience of the housekeeper, Luella, on a regular basis. I remember one night when Luella was drawing our bath and David let loose a mechanical mouse which drove Luella hysterical. Another time, David went after the maid, Peggy, with a kitchen knife and stopped just short of stabbing her. When confronted by his father he replied, "I was only teasing."

One day, David decided that we should build a club house under the house and purchased beverages and potato chips at the local store where they had account. Because it was dark, he brought a lighted candle down and tripped, leaving the candle to catch fire to the paper table cloth he had placed on a box to simulate a dining room set. We quickly exited and waited at a distance for the fire engines to arrive. Fortunately, my Uncle and Aunt were away so that we did not have to ace them over the incident. David, like his sister, went into acting and is best known for his role as Boswell in "Charlie's Angels."

Despite the many adventures in Nebraska, it was a joyous day for me when we made our way to the train station to return home and be reunited with Dad and Casey.

My father's parents, Michael and Molly Kelly, emigrated from County Cork, Ireland to Cass County, Nebraska. They purchased a farm that proved profitable and were able to send their son, Edward, to Notre Dame High School in Indiana. They were devout Irish Catholics and determined that their son receive a Catholic Education. Dad would delight in telling us stories of when he was the water boy when Knute Rockney was the coach at Notre Dame University.

It was while dad was at Notre Dame that he received the tragic news that his parents had been killed. Their Model T Ford had stalled while they were crossing over a railroad track. The president of the University, Father Scanlon, accompanied my dad home to celebrate the funeral Mass.

Dad, now an orphan, went to live with his cousins, the Fitzgerald's, in Nebraska. It was while he was attending the University of Nebraska that he met my mother. They soon began dating and my dad fell hopelessly in love with her, wanting desperately to marry her. They did not consider marriage until after graduation, however. Mother was an accomplished singer and would tell us stories of the many performers who visited their home. On one occasion, Gus Edwards, a talent scout from Hollywood tried to prevail upon my grandfather to let him take my mother back to Hollywood and launch her into an acting career. My grandfather would not hear of it.

Mother began to sing professionally and while she was performing at the Corn Husker Hotel, dad went back stage and waited until she took her final bow and exited the stage, at which time he got down on one knee and proposed to her. He asked her to elope with him and move to California. He told her that he wanted them to strike out on their own and escape the shadow of her parents, free to make their own decisions.

California was chosen because my mother's two sisters, Aunt Jessie and Aunt Betty, had moved there. Dad had inherited a large sum of money when his parents died and the farm was sold. He assured my mother that he would have no problem supporting her. I can only imagine how heart-breaking it must have been for my grandfather. The "apple of his eye" was not only opting for a private marriage ceremony, but was mocing over a thousand miles away. I'm sure my grandmother felt the pain as well. All of her daughter's had lavish church weddings, and the same was hoped for my mother, the youngest child. But, my parents were married in the parish rectory in a small, private ceremony. Immediately thereafter, they packed dup the car and set off for Fresno, California, where Aunt Betty lived. In my vivid imagination, I picture my parents speeding down the highway in a convertible with the top down, stopping at fancy hotels to dine and dance along the way.

When they arrived in Fresno, my dad bought two gas stations and promptly lost both soon thereafter when the depression hit. My brother, Edward Casey Kelly, was born on January 16, 1928—just prior to the onset of the great depression. With a new family to support, my dad took a job at the Oakland Tribune as an investigative reporter and moved his family to Oakland.

Although my father had lost all of his investments and savings, he was optimistic and knew that he would be able to support his family. I inherited this optimistic trait of my father's, and always see the "glass half full of water, not half empty."

When I look back, I see all of the gifts that I inherited from my grandparents and parents. The gift of humor. The courage to confront authority. The ability to write a book. But my most treasured inheritance, was given to me at an early age. My mother used to tell us that she and my dad would not be leaving us money, but a greater source of wealth: our faith.

2

The Twins Are Born

On April 8, 1930 at Saint Agnes Hospital in Fresno, California, the doctor entered my mother's hospital room and informed her and my father that she was expecting twins! He informed them that he could not guarantee that both mother and babies would survive the birth. To assure that my mother would live, he asked my parents to decide if the babies should be aborted.

Both of my parents in unison said, "There is no decision. The babies are to be delivered." In my imagination, I can feel for my father, who so loved my mother. It had to be heart wrenching to agree to have the babies delivered knowing that it could cost my mother's life.

Gratefully, both mother and babies survived the Caesarean birth. At 11:03 p.m. and 11:04 p.m. respectively, my sister Kay and I were "untimely lifted from our mother's womb" as Shakespeare would say. Since it was a tenuous whether or not we would live, we were baptized by one of the nurses who helped to deliver us. I was literally born into the Catholic Church.

My parents, expecting only one baby, had chosen the name Mary Kathleen if it was a girl. I was not expected so I was an "it" for three days. I didn't even have a gender. All of the telegrams sent included Mary Kathleen and it! After three days it was decided that my name would be Dorothy Jane. Dorothy for my mother and Jane for my Aunt Jane.

Mother had to remain in the hospital so dad brought us home. According to Canon Law, a baby must be baptized within 10 days of its birth so my father and members of the family attended our baptism at St. Teresa's church in Fresno. Mother could not attend since she was still hospitalized

It was a handful for dad with baby twins and a two-year-old son to care for so he was able to secure a college student, Faye, who agreed to move in and help out with the twins and housekeeping in exchange for room and board. After Faye left, dad always saw to it that mother had help caring for all of us babies.

I used to love hearing mother and dad tell us stories about when we were little. One of my favorites was the time that Kay and I got new panties with ruffles and Kay delighted in showing her panties to the people going into church on a Sunday morning. I shared this story with Kay and she informed me that it was the first new clothing she probably got, since I was bigger and so she would get my hand-me-downs.

Because my parents were both devout Catholics, I grew up in a very Catholic environment. We would never miss mass on Sunday or Holy Days of Obligaton. Every Saturday we would go to the parish church in the afternoon to go to confession. As a child, I found this extremely stressful since I would have to come up with a sin that I had committed the week before. To simplify matters, I finally came up with two sins that I was sure that I was guilty of committing: talking in class and disobeying my mother. At times, I couldn't remember when I disobeyed my mother, but I stuck to the sin anyway.

It was scary going into the dark confessional box, groping around to find the kneeler and then anxiously waiting for the priest to slide back the small window and hear him say, "Yes, my child." Gratefully, we had a formula to get us started. I would begin, "Bless my father, for I have sinned." I would make sure to include the number of times that I had committed the sin, though this number was always made up because who can remember how many times they spoke out of turn in class? With relief, I left the confessional knowing that my sins were forgiven, and that if I died I would not go to hell!

I remember once a priest said to me, "Sister Jane, I heard the confession of a little boy and was taken aback when he confessed he had committed adultery! The boy went on to explain that his mother had told him that he had been disrespectful to an adult, and that was a sin!"

Another practice that we followed every Saturday afternoon was to lay out the clothes we would wear to mass the next day, and make sure that our shoes were polished. Mother would place an offering envelope on top of our clothes to make sure we remembered to take it to Mass.

Sunday morning would find us at the children's mass where mother would sing, dad would usher, and Casey would serve at the altar. It was a tradition that dad would cook the Sunday breakfast when we came home and I can still smell the fried Linguini sausage, scrambled eggs and hot, buttered toast. Sunday was always a special day in our household.

Friday was always a meatless day, and I can remember my mother reminding me of this when I was going on a picnic with a family that was not Catholic. Mother said, "Jane, remember that if they offer you a hot dog or baked beans with meat, you must refuse." She made my peanut butter sandwiches to take for my lunch.

During the season of Lent, we would gather in the evening to pray the rosary. The rosary beads are made up of ten hail Hail Mary's known as a decade and we would take turns leading a decade of the rosary. When it came time for Casey to lead the dacade, he proceeded to simply say, "Hail Mary" without finishing the prayer. Mother would say, Casey, you are to recite the whole prayer." One evening the door bell rang and we thought the recitation would be ended. But Mother responded, "Your father will answer the door and entertain our guests until we finish the rosary." We were not saved by the bell.

Christmas was a time when we held to many family traditions. On the first Sunday in Advent, Mother would set up the crib minus the figures except for the manger. She would then set out a container of straw. Each evening we would gather and tell wheat we had done goal that day and place a straw in the manger. The goal was to place enough straw in the manger to make a comfortable bed for the baby Jesus. On Christmas Eve, mother would place the figures of Mary, Joseph, the shepherds and the animals in the crib. She would then hold up her hand with three straws and say, "Whoever picks the longest straw gets to place the infant Jesus in the crib."

When we were fast asleep on Christmas Eve, mother and dad would place a stocking at the foot of our bed. Mother was careful not to put anything edible in our stockings so that we wouldn't break our fast. In those years, you could not eat or drink anything after midnight if you wanted to receive communion the next day.

As soon as Casey woke up on Christmas morning, he would bring his stocking into our bedroom and call out, "Kay, Jane wake up!" We would eagerly show each other everything we had received. There was always a doll for Kay and I and a soldier for Casey, as well as yoyos, marbles, and other small trinkets.

On Christmas morning we would attend Mass and, as usual, mother would sing, dad would usher, and Casey would serve at the alter. One year, they were all scheduled for a different Mass. This meant a long delay before we were allowed to see what Santa Clause had left us under the tree. I soon learned that there were drawbacks to being Catholic!

Another Catholic ritual that we observed was to have the priest come to the house, bless it, and enthrone the picture of the Sacred Heart of Jesus. The blessing was always followed with cake and ice cream. Every time we moved we would remind mother that the hose needed to be blessed!

At age five, we were enrolled in Saint Elizabeth's School, which was run by Mission San Jose Dominicans. I remember standing around the classroom on the first day while the Sister called our name to be seated. When she called Dorothy Kelly I did not move, since I was always called Jane. The rule was that you were to be called by your first name, and it wasn't until I reached the third grade that my teacher graciously agreed to call me Jane.

On the first day of school, the first graders had only a half day of school so mother didn't come to get us until dismissal time. When mother didn't arrive to pick us up, we began to cry and the principal took us to Casey's room where we sat on the bench seat on either side of him. Most brothers would have died, sitting with their younger sisters, but Casey loved us and always felt proud of us. He always boasted that he had twin sisters.

During this time we lived on Harrington Street in Oakland. It was a small house, but we loved it because there was a hill in the back that was perfect for sliding down on an old cardboard box. The house was a distance from the school, so mother would drive us until we were old enough to walk on our own. Mother's last words to us before heading off to school every day were always, "Don't dilly dally on the way."

The instruction fell on deaf ears because we would take our time looking into the store windows on Fruitvale Avenue, and would stop to talk to the shoe shine man who would often give us a jawbreaker. Inevitably we would arrive after the first bell and would have to report to the principal, Sister Claudia, who threatened to give us an alarm clock so that we wouldn't be late. We assured her we would never be late again, because if she gave us an alarm clock Mother would know that we had taken our sweet time to get school.

I used to hate going to school because I would miss my mother terribly. Mother would go to Mass at 6:40 a.m and I would beg her to me go with her, but she felt it was too early for me and made me wait to accompany her until I was in the fourth grade. From that time on, I attended morning Mass daily.

By this time we had moved to Thirty-Third Avenue, which was only a few blocks from Saint Elizabeth's School and Church. The house seemed like a mansion compared to the cottage on Harrington. I remember the day that mother and dad took us to see the house and warned us not to go on the walkway in the backyard as it had cracks that could cause a fall. I slipped out the back door and headed straight for the walkway where I promptly tripped and broke my arm.

Not wanting to tell my parents, I kept my arm clutched tightly under my jacket. It was while we were at dinner that mother noticed that I was white as a sheet and asked if I was in pain. I burst out crying and told her what had happened. All five of us climbed into the car and drove to Highland Hospital. My arm was placed in a wooden splint and I was told to return the next day for a cast.

When dad took me back to the hospital the following day, we were surprised that they ushered me into a hospital room and had me get into bed. Dad went in search of the doctor to see why I was being admitted. It turned out they though I was the child who was scheduled to have her appendix taken out! I hated every moment of that hospital visit and couldn't wait to leave, cast and all.

About eight days after I had the cast put on, I was in the process of making a scooter with one of my skates and while I was attempting to hammer a nail in, I broke the cast. Mother took me to have a new cast put on, where the doctor kindly urged me to use a hammer the next time. Two weeks later, my brother and I decided to run two rails down from the garage and make a runway using my wagon as the vehicle. My brother, being a gentleman, said that women should go first. So into the wagon I went, while Casey held on to it. When he released his hold, the rails, the wagon, and I all went crashing to the ground. Back to the doctor I went for a new cast, this time being told to avoid any situation that could potentially harm the cast.

Growing up, my brother and I were very close. I often hung out with him and his friends, while Kay played with girl friends. When Casey and his friends built a club house where they could play strip poker, I begged, "Please, Casey, let me play poker with you in the club house." Casey said, "Jane, only if you put paper clips in your pockets so that yo won't have to forfeit any clothing." I can still picture how excited I was to crawl into the club house where we sat around an overturned box as the cards were dealt. Gratefully, I had the paper clips in my pocket, since I rarely won.

My brother knew how to get me to do his bidding. When he became constipated, mother gave him a small container of milk of magnesia. After she left the room, Casey said that he would give me a nickel if I drank it for him. When he still wasn't having any luck, mother would give him a second dose. I was getting rich and mother couldn't understand was Casey was still constipated and I had diarrhea!

On some nights, Casey would come into our bedroom after mother and dad had gone to bed and ask me to sneak downstairs and make him a peanut butter and jelly sandwich. My reward would be that he would tell us a story and illustrate as he went along. He was a great artist and I can still picture the vivid characters that he would draw. It was invariably a mystery to be solved by a detective.

In the sixth grade, while at the movies on December 8th, the sound was turned off and the announcement was made that Pearl Harbor was attacked and we had declared war on Japan. Our way of life was changed. We were subject to blackouts and exposed to the loud siren that warned us to turn our lights out. Each time there was a dread that this might be the real thing.

I'll never forget the time when I was at a dance overseen by the nuns when the siren went off. The Sister had the boys sit on one side of the dance hall and the girls on the other. We had great fun sneaking over to the boy's side until the all clear sign was given, the lights went back on, and the game was up!

We were also introduced to a rationing system that limited the goods we were able to purchase. Meat was rationed but our butcher never took the coupon from us. He didn't want to lose a sale. The same thing happened when we went to buy shoes.. The hardest part for me was rationing butter. I was forced to use margarine on my toast. Though my mother would mix the margarine with food coloring and shape it to resemble a cube of butter, I could taste the difference.

Because my father was Four F (He was forty and had three children), he had to get a wartime job. He got work at Bethlehem Steel in San Francisco. So off to San Francisco, we went.

3

San Francisco Bound

The day had finally arrived in June of 1943 when we would move to San Francisco. The weather matched my feelings. It was overcast and gloomy. I was leaving all of my friends and the school I had attended for six years.

To add to the pain, we could not take our dog, Lucky with us. I tried to smuggle Lucky onto the moving van by putting her in my mother's empty cedar chest. However, when I went to look for Lucky after we arrived in San Francisco, I only came up with an empty cedar chest! Mother tried to console me by assuring me that Lucky had gone to a loving family. For the first time in my life, we were without a dog.

San Francisco proved to be a whole new experience. We no longer lived in a house but a flat on Clayton Street just three blocks from Saint Ignatius Church. Our quarters were on the top flat and to open the door you had to push on a lever at the top of the stairs. We had great fun with the lever. One of us would go downstairs and ring the bell then the other would push the lever. Mother soon put a stop to our fun, informing us that it was not a toy.

Our first evening, mother walked us down to Hayes Street to get ice cream cones, and I was intrigued by the fog. I at first thought it was rain, but mother explained that it was fog because we lived close to the ocean. You could hear the fog horns in the distance and I always enjoyed walking in the fog and listening to the horns. To this day, I still miss the fog and the sound of the foghorns in the evening.

My first trip to downtown San Francisco was to go to the Emporium on Market Street. Mother took Kay and me to buy coats because the weather in San Francisco was so chilly. I was overcome by the width of Market Street and the countless highrise buildings. The atmosphere was charged with activity. People seemed to be rushing to get to where they were going.

I found San Francisco to be a fascinating city. Unlike Oakland, there was so much to see and do. We lived just one block up from the Panhandle, which led into Golden Gate Park. There we could visit the DeYoung Museum and the Hall of Flowers. Our house was only a short distance from the ocean and the ruins of the Sutro Baths as well as the historic Cliff House.

Much of our time was spent at Play Land across from the beach. It boasted carnival rides, a fun house and games. On other days we would venture to Fisherman's Wharf to watch the cooks boiling crabs in huge tanks along the walkway. We never passed without purchasing a small container of fresh crab meat, accompanied by San Francisco's famous French bread.

Shortly after moving, Mother took us to enroll in school. She was thrilled that Casey would be attending Saint Ignatius High School because it was run by the Jesuit order of priests. She grew up in a Jesuit Parish in Lincoln and her brothers attended Jesuit High Schools. This meant that Casey could attend Saint Ignatius High School.

Kay and I were enrolled at Saint Agnes Elementary School, which was run by Presentation Sisters. Little did I dream that I would one day enter the Presentation Congregation. I remember well the day that mother took us to register at Saint Agnes. Sister Rosina interviewed us and she had a wonderful sense of humor. We laughed our way through the process.

Sister shared the story of the time that she and her brother were playing with matches and the drapes in the living room caught fire. They went into the kitchen to tell their mother what they had done, and took their time in searching for the right words. In the meantime the drapes were in flames! I had never experienced a nun with such a sense of humor. It was repeated when we registered at the rectory and Father McCabe took our information. He had a sense of humor that matched Sister Rosina's.

On the first day of school, Kay and I met our seventh grade teacher, Sister Francis. She was not only beautiful; she had a gentle way about her. She had a great rapport with her students. On cold mornings she would tell us to bring a thermos of hot chocolate, which we would drink together before heading out to recess. She was so human.

I'll never forget the day that we were to learn the results of our reading test and Sister said that she would call us by name according to the one that had the highest score. When she called my name, I was stunned. For my first six years, I did poorly in school because I hated school. I can remember when my fourth grade teacher told my mother I couldn't even copy correctly from the blackboard! To me it didn't make sense why we were copying something that was in our textbook. When I brought this up with the teacher, she informed me that I should not question. "Just do as you are told, Jane." I did, but not successfully.

Another time I misspelled the word "during" and spent the recess time coping the word 100 times! To this day, I cannot spell the word without looking it up. I just finished doing so. I vowed that if ever I became a teacher, I would never have a child copy a word 100 times.

I couldn't believe it when Sister Rosina called out my name. I had received 100% on the test! This convinced me that I was not dumb. From that day on, I became an A student.

It seemed to be my fate to spend most of my time sitting outside of the principal's office. My talking and humor in class were not appreciated by my teacher. Kay would fill me in on what I missed in class, but she must not have been all innocence herself. I remember the principal, Sister Albious, called us both to the office and said, "Since you enrolled in school there have been nothing but problems!"

Once a year we took diocesan tests, which rated the schools. Gratefully, I thought I was off the hook since I was seated outside the principals once again and didn't think I would be allowed to take the test. Not so. The test was handed to me and, with my folder balanced on my lap, I proceeded to answer all of the question. Undoubtedly, they wanted my score.

The seventh grade found me interested in boys, and Kay and I gravitated to the eighth grade students. The seventh graders were mostly short and of course you were never found going around with a boy shorter than you.

Barn dances were the in thing at that time. Plaid shirts and jeans were the dress cod at the dances. I remember the time Kay and I were all set to go when dad stopped us. He did not think it appropriate to go out dressed in jeans and plaid shirts, so we went back to the bedroom and changed. We put the jeans and shirts in a bag and got passed our dad!

It's a wonder that my eighth grade teacher didn't have a nervous breakdown. We were a notorious class for causing all kind of trouble. On one occasion, we were practicing in church for graduation and decided that we would all click our thumb nails together. To say the least, the sound was nerve wracking. Our teacher threatened us with no graduation if we did not stop immediately. All of us were anxious to graduate so we stopped immediately.

The time soon came to choose a high School. Kay and I wanted to go to Lowell, which was a co-ed, public high school. My brother was adamant that we should go to a girl's Catholic High School. He must have made out with some Lowell girls! What eventually made our decision to go to the Presentation Academy occurred when it was announced that there would be no school for girls who attended an open house at the Academy. Welcoming a day off, we attended the open house. They must have done a snow job on us, because by the end of the day, we decided to go to Presentation. We called it "Prisontation."

The Kelly Twins made their mark on the Presentation High School freshman class of 1944. In a class of over 100 students, I was elected class president and Kay vice president.

Soon after, I became close friends with Doe Mahoney. We shared many an escapade that landed us in the principal's life. What she didn't think of, I did. My history of spending ample time sitting outside the principal's office certainly followed me into high school!

The first day of our Sophomore year I talked Doe into helping me sell tickets to the swimming pool on the roof to the Freshmen. It was 25 cents a ticket. Our financial venture was short lived. The Sisters discovered what we were up to, and we had to refund all the money and spend an hour in the study hall after school.

Doe came up with a great idea for getting out of Latin class. We should rub our arms with an orange solution in the photography room and the tell our Latin teacher, Sister Canice, that the solution was acid and would burn our skin if we did not wash it off immediately. She ordered us immediately to go to the girl's bathroom and wash it off. We gained thirty minutes out of class.

It was this same Sister Canice who had entered the convent from Ireland at the age of thirteen. She was naïve when it came to boys. According to her, we should carry a telephone book with us when we went out on a date lest we would have to sit on a boy's lap. I could picture myself going out on a date with the San Francisco telephone book tucked under my arm!

If we talked in class, we were sent out to the corridor and made to kneel in front of the Blessed Mother's statue praying for forgiveness. The Virgin Mary and I became very close during this time.

The principal and the teachers came to the conclusion that they could no longer tolerate Doe and myself together in the high school. One of us had to transfer. It was decided that Doe would transfer to Saint Rose, and I would remain at Presentation. How I missed my partner in crime! I now had to go solo with my antics.

It was during my Sophomore and Junior years that I was going steady with three boys. John from St. Mary's in Morago, Darrell from Washington High School and David from Bellerman. Each time I went out, I had to be sure I was wearing the right ring.

I remember when I went to meet Mother Carthagh, the Major Superior of the Sisters of the Presentation, and I forgot to remove John's ring. In the course of the interview she remarked on the ring. Not wanting her to know that I was going steady, I was quick to say that it belonged to my cousin and he was letting me wear it for a time. Feeling guilty for having lied to Mother Carthagh, I later called Sister Consuela, who was sponsoring me, and told her that I lied to Mother Carthagh.

She laughed and said, "Jane, she didn't believe you."

I was terribly excited the day that David asked me go to the Bellarmine High School's Junior prom. Bing Crosby's sons attended Bellarmine, and two of them were at the prom. I felt like I was mingling with celebrities. After the prom, we came back to San Francisco where I snuck up the back stairs so as not to awaken my parents, and changed my clothes so we could go down town for breakfast and on to 6:00 a.m. Mass.

David and I spent almost every Sunday together. He loved snakes and we would go to the zoo where he would actually be permitted to remove a snake from its cage and hold it. I have to admit that snakes were not my favorite animal!

Several years ago I was taping a segment at the local radio station and the engineer approached me and said, "Sister Jane you don't recognize me do you?" It was David and he pulled out his wallet, which contained the picture that was taken at his Junior prom. He went on to say that he never came to love anyone more than me. David shared that he was married and that they adopted five children. They never were able to have children. How astounding that, after all these years, we would come to live in Mendocino County!

Darrell had a Model T Ford with a rumble seat. We took many drives out to China beach to bathe in the sun. On once occasion, Darrel took me to the olive ranch that his parents owned and graciously picked an olive off a tree and offered it to me. It proved to be the bitterest taste I had ever experienced. It almost ended our friendship right there. His parents later informed me that you never eat an olive until it has been cured.

Because the nation was at war and there was a shortage of man power, it was easy for young people to get jobs. I lied about my age and secured a job in the stock room at Penney's. I remember the thrill when I received my first pay envelope that contained $7.50!

My knack for getting into trouble carried over into the workplace. I would chase the stock boys around the stock room, laughing the whole time. My behavior was brought to the attention of my supervisor and I was called to the office where two other employees were seated. The manager informed us that he would have to let two of us go. One of the employees was a woman who obviously needed the job, so the other teenager and urged the manager to let us go. The grateful woman said that she would pray that we find other jobs. Her prayers quickly paid off as we crossed the street to the Emporium, filled out applications, and were told to come back the next Saturday at 9:00 a.m.

Every Saturday morning I would go up to the employment office to find out which department I was assigned to that day. Having lied about my age, I would inform the supervisor that I was late and didn't have time to get my work permit. I carried this off for two year!

My first assignment was on the first floor where I sold handkerchiefs. I soon found out that I was a natural at securing a sale. Since the woman I was working for earned a commission based on her sales, I would ring my sales on her register once I had reached my goal on mine. I did this in each department that I worked in. The ladies loved me for it and would often bring me a box of candy.

During my Sophomore year I became close friends with Joanne O'Shea. She was a year ahead of me and we met during the time I spent in the Physics Lab in my private study period. Sister Mary Clare was her cousin and Joanne would come to the Lab to visit with Sister. She wielded a positive influence on me.

We both worked at the Emporium and would arrange to have the same lunch break. On Friday's we would have dinner together and then make a Holy Hour at old St. Mary's. Saturday night was reserved for dating. Sundays we would go to two or three movies together. To this day Sister Joanne loves movies. She entered the convent the year after I did.

Sister Mary Consuela played a significant role in my decision to enter the convent. She taught me photography and I would often meet with her after classes and help out in the Lab. Many a Saturday I would spend with her cleaning or developing film.

It was while I was Social Director that I got into selling tickets once again. This time it was raffle tickets for a turkey. The custom was that every feast of the Presentation, the students would give a gift of money and a decorated cake to the sisters. I decided that we would top any amount of money that had been given in the past. We would present the Sisters with a thousand dollars as well as two decorated cakes! To raise the money, I would have raffle tickets printed and ask each student to sell at least one book which was worth five dollars. Since there were over four hundred students, that would net us two thousand dollars. We would still make well over a thousand dollars in the event that some students failed to sell a book. The prize would be a turkey.

Eileen Crummy knew a printer and he printed the tickets for thirty dollars. The tickets arrived on a Wednesday and I asked Sister Consuela if I could put them in a cabinet in the physics lab until I could distribute them to the students. She agreed. Later that day, I got called to the Mother House. Mother Carthagh wanted to see me. I was baffled. What would she want to see me for? After greeting me, Mother Carthagh proceeded to tell me that it was illegal to sell raffle tickets. What was I going to do? We owed thirty dollars for the tickets, which couldn't be returned. That night I came up with the answer.

The next day, I bought four hundred small white envelopes. The plan was to give each student an envelope, which was to be returned with three dollars. I asked Sister Olivia, our principal, if I could call a Student Body meeting without any of the Sisters present. She agreed and I held the meeting with only lay teachers present. The envelopes were distributed along with the directions. Three dollars were to be placed in the envelope and the envelope given to the girls on traffic duty. The envelopes poured in and were opened and counted. I arranged with Sister Consuela, to take the money each afternoon to be placed in a safe at the Mother House.

Two days before the Feast Day, we were four hundred dollars. Again I requested a meeting with the students without the sisters present. I informed the girls that no one would leave the auditorium until I collected the money. "I will accept car tokens, lunch tickets and gold teeth if necessary." Within a half hour we raised the money.

The morning of the Feast Day, Sister Consuela had me come to the office and handed me a thousand dollar bill. I had never seen a thousand dollar bill in my life nor have I seen one since. With due honors we presented the Sisters with the money, two decorated cakes and a bouquet of flowers to boot!

PART II

4

Preparing to Enter the Convent

Just prior to entering the convent, I had a most unusual experience.

I was at a dance on Haight Street and, while I was dancing, a vision appeared just over the right shoulder of my partner. It was the image of Christ on the cross. I was so moved that I abruptly left the dance and made my way up to Saint Ignatius Church.

In those days churches were always open. The smell of incense filled the dimly lit church. I slowly made my way up to the altar where the votive candles were placed beneath the Blessed Mother's statue. Rummaging in my pockets, I could only find a fifty cent coin. Reluctantly, I dropped the coin into the slot and lit a candle praying that if God wanted me to enter the convent, He would have to make it happen! I felt the prayer was worth fifty cents.

The following Monday morning I was summoned to Sister Annetta's office. Undoubtedly, Sister Consuela had told her of my desire to enter the Order. After greeting me, she ushered me to a chair and proceeded to tell me why she asked to see me.

"Jane, Sister Consuela informed me that you wish to enter the convent. You undoubtedly will be elected Student Body President and it wouldn't be fair to the students if you were elected and then entered in your Senior year. They would have to go through the process of electing a new President. I strongly urge you to enter on April 13th."

God surely answered my prayer in record time! Having convinced me, I told Sister that I would ask my parents that night.

That evening, I waited until my father came home from work and went into the kitchen where mother was preparing dinner.

I blurted out, "Mother, I want to enter the convent in April." She smiled and told me that she had always been sure that I would become a nun. Mother was happy that I had decided on Presentation. She felt my other choice, Mission San Jose Dominicans, was more strict.

"You must go in and tell your father."

Dad was sitting in the living room reading the evening paper and smoking his pipe as usual before dinner. Once again, I blurted out that I wanted to enter the convent in April. His immediate response was, "Jane, aren't you happy at home?"

"Yes, but I love God and want to serve Him," I said. Dad reminded me that I would miss my Junior and Senior Prom as well as graduation. "However, if this is what you want, you have my blessing."

You can imagine the dinner conversation that night. My brother, Casey, was delighted. He would often tease me and say, "Jane, get thee to a nunnery." I hated when he said that and once, in a burst of anger, threw a bottle opener after him! Mother was right when she said that I would have to learn how to control my temper.

Kay, my twin sister, was going to miss me as I would she. In our sixteen, going on seventeen, years we had never been separated.

Mother and dad discussed when the family would be informed. It was decided that we would have a party just before Christmas and invite the Reed cousins. We all agreed that Aunt Betty would be thrilled with my decision. She was a very religious woman, never missed daily Mass, and was even known to go to all of the Masses on Sunday!

Having been given a list of the things that I needed before entering the convent, mother and I went shopping. Our first stop was the shoe store. Since I was embarrassed because the shoes looked like men's, I told the clerk that I was buying them for a nun who had my same she size.

It was then on to the Emporium to buy yards of gingham for work aprons. The sales lady wanted to know if I was decorating my bedroom in gingham since I was purchasing so many yards.

There was need for a roman collar to go with the outfit so we went to Kaufers, a religious store. The gentleman there wanted to know if I was going to play priest. I could have shot him. While we were there, mother pointed to a table of books on display and told me that I could have whatever one I wished. It didn't take a minute to decide. I chose the book on the Maryknoll Sisters.

Because they were a Missionary Order, I had a desire to enter Maryknoll. However someone told me that you had to become a nurse to enter. Given my aversion to hospitals, I knew that I could not become a nurse. Years later, I met the Provincial for the Maryknoll Sisters and she informed me that you did not have to be a nurse to enter. It seems God did not want me to enter Maryknoll.

When I went to get measured for my Postulant outfit, I ran into Janet Harris, a classmate. The next day, I met her on the school corridor and she came up and said, "Jane, you are entering also?" I pushed her up against the wall and told her that I would kill her if she told anyone! My tactic was effective because she shared the knowledge with no one.

When word got out that one of the Kelly twins was going to enter, everyone thought it was Kay. It couldn't be Jane, they thought. She is too wild! Kay, to this day, claims that her grades went up because of that rumor.

A few days before Christmas, Mother invited the Reeds to a party celebrating my entrance. To my amazement the tree was decorated with tooth brushes. We were asked to bring a 6 month supply of tooth brushes and toothpaste to last our six months as a postulant. (Probation period before receiving the habit).

After everyone had arrived at the party, Kay came out dressed in my postulant outfit along with the "nun's shoes"! Everyone laughed, but I was irate. I demanded that Kay remove the outfit.

That night proved nostalgic. My parents and Uncle Dick and Aunt Betty regaled us with stories of when we were growing up. We watched home movies on an eight millimeter camera. There were pictures of the Reeds and ourselves at Santa Cruz Beach. The shot that moved me most was when they had a close up of dad teaching me to swim. I never did learn.

The night before I entered the convent, Joanne O'Shea spent the night. She was to enter in June, just after her graduation.

The next day, my brother and dad walked me to the convent on Turk and Masonic. Mother had just come home from the hospital and could not accompany me. It was just as well since I broke down in sobs when I left her. We walked up the tile stairs and rang the bell. I could hear it resounding throughout the building.

Mother Gertrude, the Novice Mistress, greeted us at the door and ushered us into the Presentation parlor. She took me upstairs and I changed into my postulant outfit and net veil and came down to say goodbye to my brother and dad. I wouldn't see them for a month, and then only for two hours. During this period, we only saw our family on Visiting Sunday which was the last Sunday of the month. Our parents were the ones who would pay the price. We would become so caught up in our new life that the time lapse would not be a problem.

I embraced dad and Casey with tears on both sides, and saw them to the door. My convent days were to begin.

5

My Postulent Days

After Casey and my dad left, having brought me to the convent, Mother Gertrude, the Novice Mistress, took me upstairs to meet the Sisters.

I was introduced to each novice and postulant and assigned an "angel." Every postulant was given an "angel" who was to instruct us in the practices and the rules of the novitiate. Sister Concepta was to be my angel. She showed me to my room and informed me that we refer to our rooms as "cells." Upon leaving our cells in the morning, we were not to go back to them during the day without permission. I was quickly ushered into the mode of asking permission of the Novice Mistress for everything, even permission to write a letter.

From our cells we went to the dining room, which I was told we call the refectory. Interestingly, when the colonists wanted to punish criminals, they placed them in a monastery setting, in hopes of rehabilitating them. Hence you got the words "cell" and "refectory."

I remember in the early sixties someone wrote a book highlighting the similarities among Mental Hospitals, Prisons, the Military and Religious Orders. Sisters were incensed. For me it was right on target. When you enter any one of the institutes, you are given a uniform, a number and your hair is cut. The only difference in the convent is that the doors are not locked and you are free to walk through them at any time.

Each sister was assigned a place in the refectory. I was shown to mine and instructed that the drawer contained my dishes and silverware. In the corner of my drawer, I noticed a small packet of sheets from a telephone book. The sheets were to be used to wipe the butter or any grease from our knife or fork. Sister Concepta went on to explain that we wash our dishes at the table in a bowl that held soapy water and a small mop. It was a great day when automatic dishwashers were installed but that wasn't until years later!

To facilitate the drying of our dishes we had a large napkin which was changed every week. I found it hard to believe that we would wash our dishes at our place in a bowl that had made its way down the long refectory table. Its point of origin was the Professed Sisters table. You can imagine the color of the water by the time it reached me!

On leaving the refectory, we made our way to the bathrooms. One room held the bathroom stalls and the other the bath tubs. I was handed a bathing garment that resembled a long slip. It was to be worn while you bathed. No way was I going to take a bath wearing that garment! I simply dunked it into the tub and then rang it out and hung it out on the clothesline. No one was the wiser.

This was not my only infraction of the rules.

We were to change our stockings once a week and send them to the laundry.

I would wash mine out each night and pray that they would dry. If not, I would fold them, damp side out, and place them in the wardrobe. To a person who was used to taking two baths a day and changed her clothing, socks included, on a daily basis, the whole thing was shocking. They say that, "Cleanliness is next to Godliness," and I was just trying to get closer to Godliness!

Another rule was that we were not to go into each others cell. I recall when my friend, Joanne, came into my cell to show me how to pin my veil. She no sooner sat down on my chair when it collapsed and broke into pieces! Not wishing to tell the Novice Mistress that Joanne had broken the chair, I took the pieces and made a reparation for breaking the chair. I was humiliated when I took the broken chair down to dispose of it. I met some of my high school classmates coming into the convent and blushed with the broken chair in my hands, unable to speak to them.

As novices, we were not to speak except at the half hour recreation period in the afternoon and in the evening. The only exception was when the Major Superior rang a bell announcing a "Tu Autom," which meant we could speak during the meal.

The recreation period consisted of being paired off with two other sisters as we walked up and down the courtyard sharing our events of the day or exchanging humorous stories. On rare occasions we might play volley ball. We were never paired off in two's lest we develop a preferential friendship. We called them P.F's.

During evening recreation, we sat around the Novitiate table, darning our socks and addressing our words to the Novice Mistress who sat at the head of the table.

I had been ushered into a world of silence! It was a whole new life style for me.

The only time we listened to music was on Christmas and Easter. One exception was when the rosary was on radio. We would go down to the guest parlor and pray the rosary. The narrator was always either Bing Crosby or Perry Como.

This particular night I announced that it was Perry Como, but Mother Gertrude corrected me and said that it was Bing Crosby. At the end of the program it was announced that Perry Como was the narrator! No words were exchanged but I had the quiet satisfaction of hearing tht it was, indeed, Perry Como.

This radical change in my life took its toll on my physical as well as my mental health. One night we were served liver, onions and bacon. I remember when my dad said that he would pay me ten cents for every bite of liver I ate. I had tried to hide the bites under the table but to no avail. My father discovered them and as the saying goes, "I never made a dime on the deal."

Since we were to take a serving of anything that came down the table, I dutifully took a portion of the liver and ate it. That night, Sister Concepta woke up Mother Gertrude and said that I was delirious and hallucinating. The next thing I knew there were all of these faces peering down on me asking if I recognized them. It was Sisters Consuela, Annetta, Clare and Mother Olivia. When I did not respond, Mother Olivia called the convent doctor, Dr. Firpo. He came and pumped my stomach and informed Mother Olivia that the liver I ate that night was poison to my system. I should never eat liver. Now, I know why I could never stomach liver. Our bodies know when we shouldn't eat certain foods.

Since I was still out of it, they moved me to a small cell at the end of the corridor. The sisters in the Novitiate thought I went home. I reappeared two weeks later, much to the relief of the Sisters.

Having always been an avid reader, it was difficult for me to be reduced to simply reading the thin book on the Catechism of the Vows and a book on the vow of obedience by a Spanish Spiritual writer Rodriguez that we were given as postulants. Boring to say the least! I finally went to the Novice Mistress complaining of the lack of reading material. The limited reading material left me unchallenged, I told her.

She sent me down to the Major Superior, Mother Carthagh. Entering the office, I knelt at her desk, as was the custom when speaking to a auperior, and explained to her that I had read extensively before I entered and wanted to read a book that would expand my knowledge.

She was impressed that I had read "Mysteries of the Christ" by Don Marmion. Gratefully, she gave me a book on the Eucharist and told me that she would give the same book to Sister Claude, another novice, and we could spend thirty minutes each Friday sharing what we had read. This was just the first of many times that I would be sent down to Mother Carthagh to have a question answered.

During one of our lectures, Mother Gertrude made the statement that the priest takes the place of Christ during the Mass. I asked, "If Christ is still alive how can the priest take his place?"

Once again I was sent down to Mother Carthagh to receive an answer. She explained that the priest did not take the place of Christ but was a physical presence of Christ who was no longer physically present in a body.

In June of my postulant year, the congregation held a General Chapter at which time a new Mother General was to be elected. Since all of the cells at the Mother House would be needed to house the professed sisters attending, the Novititae was sent to Moss Beach, our vacation house. The house was small and had only two small bathrooms and two bedrooms. To accommodate the thirty of us, Sister Annetta arranged to have quansat huts delivered to house us during the duration. Unfortunately, the quansat huts that contained the showers and toilets never arrived. We were given five minutes each to wash up in one of the bathrooms but not allowed to take a bath or a shower. Mother Gertrude and Sister Claude slept in the cots by the door and would, with the aid of a flashlight, accompany any sister that had to use the bathroom during the night.

It was during this "vacation," that I heard myself called "sister," by someone outside the convent for the first time. We were taking a hike up the hill when it started to rain. A car pulled up beside us and the driver called out, "Sisters, can I give you a ride?" I felt a chill go through me, until after we declined and I hear his companion say, "They're robbing the cradle now!"

When the day came that we were to return to the Mother House, I rejoiced. Finally, I could take a bath and wash off the week's worth of accumulated dirt. Godliness at last!

During our absence, our High School principal, Sister Olivia, had been elected Mother General. It was bittersweet for me. I was delighted over her election but sad to lose her as our English teacher. She made literature come alive. I can still hear her voice as she read the works of Sir Walter Scott to us. Later, when I was sent to her office because I had worn out the two pairs of shoes I had brought with me upon entering, she exclaimed, "Sister, you must work hard and move fast!"

The time was nearing when my six-month period of waiting to receive the habit was nearing. Because there was a postulant who received the habit in October, I was fearful that we would be delayed in receiving the habit in November. Not so. The date was set and we would receive the habit on November 23, 1947.

There were three of us. Patricia Madrugal, Patricia Barnicle and myself all entered at the same time so we would receive the habit together. We were allowed to list three names that we would like to be known by. I chose Edward, my father's name, Eusebia my sixth grade teacher and Redempta. I just liked the name Redempta which was short for redemption. We had been redeemed from sin by Christ when He became incarnated and I related to that mystery in the life of Jesus.

6

My Days as a Novice

The day I had dreamed of for six months finally dawned. I was to be clothed in the habit of a nun with cincture and rosary beads! On the day of our Reception, we were dressed in bridal dresses and veils. We were considered brides of Christ.

This reminds me of a story about a man who underwent a life threatening surgery and when he came to the Sister nurse told him that she had good news and bad news. The man said, "Sister, give me the good news first."

She responded, "Your surgery was a complete success." "The bad news is that the cost of the surgery is tremendous. Do you have a relative that could help you pay the cost?"

"Sister, the only relative is my sister who is a nun and she doesn't have a husband."

"Oh, but she does," replied the Sister. "She is married to Christ."

"Fine," replied the man," send the bill to my brother-in-law."

On the morning of our reception, Sisters Consuela and Clare took pictures of us in our wedding dresses. It occurred to me that this would be the last picture taken of me in secular clothes. From this day forward I would be clothed in the habit that exposed only my face and hands.

Family members were invited to the procession, and I can still picture my mom, dad and Kay sitting in the first row. Casey stood at the alter as the server. We processed in, accompanied by beautiful organ music played by Sister Mary Annunciata. As we approached the alter, the Sister who was sponsoring us accompanied us and carried our habit. We knelt as the priest blessed our habits and prayed over us.

The Sisters led us out of the chapel and to a cell just outside of the chapel to don our habit and cut our hair. It was a dramatic moment to see all of my curls fall to the floor, but bittersweet as I realized I would never again have to deal with my hair!

Dressed in the habit, the three of us lined up in front of the chapel to be given our new names. I didn't catch mine and asked my companions if they heard what it was. The response was negative so I didn't learn what it was until the priest called me by name. "Sister Mary Catherine Laboure' come forward." I had no clue as to who Catherine Laboure' was. I had never heard of the saint. As it turned out she was a Sister of Charity who had just been beatified, which was a step away from sainthood. My father later asked me how I got the name. I stretched the truth and told him it was the closest to Kathleen after my sister, Kay.

Incensed that I was not given one of the names I requested, I went to Mother Gertrude and demanded to know why I was told to list three names when not one of them was given to me. Once again, I was sent to the Major Superior to have my question answered. She told me that Mother Carthagh had prayed to Blessed Catherine Laboure' for postulants, promising to name the first postulant, Catherine Laboure'.

I endured many of the names that the children would call me when I went out to teach. The most offensive was Catherine Lavatory, while my Sister friends called me Laughing Cabaret due to my ability to cause laughter wherever I went. When I was principal and ordered a stamp with my name on it to affix to the report cards, it was too long to fit on the card! When the package arrived, I thought it was a map rack.

Having been received, I entered what they called the "Canonical Year." We were not to have classes in secular subjects. The year was spent in deepening our spiritual life.

Each morning we would rise at 5:25 a.m., leap out of bed and kiss the floor. I'm not sure what that practice was all about. However, we learned later that many of the practices that we were taught had been introduced by an over zealous Sister! For instance, we were to cut our slice of bread in the form of a cross—a practice which Mother Olivia put an end to. She informed us that it was customary to break the bead before eating it. So, we began breaking our bread and putting jam on it before eating it. One of the novices, however, kept forgetting to break her bread so we were served more bread and jam until all had mastered the task. I thought that I would be perfectly happy never eating another piece of bread after that.

Another Novice was making the stations of the cross and slipped on the newly waxed floor and glided to the next station. A postulant who witnessed this thought that's what you do at the seventh station. You glide to the eighth. It took her some time to master the practice.

It was the custom that each of the Novices took turns ringing the bell to awaken the other Sisters every morning. At 5:25 you were to begin ringing the bell and proceed down each corridor to make sure the Sisters heard it. When it came my turn, being a heavy sleeper, I didn't hear the alarm go off. I was awakened by the sound of someone else ringing the bell! As penance, I had to do it for the week. To make sure I heard the alarm, I placed in on a dish in hopes that it would amplify the sound. It did in fact amplify the sound to the point that it alone could have awakened the Sisters!

The "Great Silence" began at 9:00 p.m. and was also announced by the bell ringer. We were not to speak unless it was an emergency. For the Novitiate, it was a signal that all lights were to be turned off.

It was a tradition that on the Feast of The Holy Innocents that a Sister in the novitiate was elected the Major Superior for that day. Inevitably the first act was to bring out the Sees candies which were shelved in the wardrobe.

When it came to mealtime, she would sit at the head of the refectory table and ring the little bell that announced a "Tu autum" (to speak). Sister Dennis, who was the newly elected Major Superior for the day, blew a whistle instead of ringing the little bell. Most of the Sisters jumped out of their seats! We were also given permission to speak whenever and wherever we wished. Mother Gertrude intervened and informed us that we were to speak only in the Novitiate room. We were given permission to turn on the radio and listen to music, but again Mother Gertrude modified that permission, telling us that she would monitor what we were listening to.

Throughout the day we were often in trouble following the lead of Sister Dennis and I vowed that if I were elected all of the novitiate would go to the laundry that day so we would not get into trouble. The day arrived and I did just that. However, I did make sure that the Sees candy was put out.

We were to make our reparations if we had something to accuse ourselves of in the refectory every morning. You would go to the center of the refectory and kneel down and address your accusation to the Major Superior who would then give you a penance. Every Monday after I was the server, I would accuse myself of not seeing to the needs of my Sisters. The Novice Mistress said that it was expected of you. I did not feel that I had neglected the needs of my Sisters. I would even respond immediately when Sister Patrick Rupert would tap er fingeron ther tea cup to signal that she wanted more tea. If you delayed she would begin in wave her handkerchief. I didn't think it was right for me to accuse myself of something I was not guilty of doing and went down to tell this to Mother Olivia. "Sister, if you feel you are not guilty then you shouldn't make a reparation." That afternoon she assembled the Sisters of the novitiate and instructed us to only make a reparation if we felt we were guilty of an infraction.

My career of bringing change to established practices had been sowed. It would come to full bloom when I was appointed a Superior at the early age of twenty-nine!

Because whoever sat next to me in the refectory would burst into laughter at my remarks, I was constantly moved to another place. They finally ran out of places for me to sit so I ended up sitting next to the Novice Mistress, Sister Gertrude. Little laughter emerged. The perfect place had been found. I was so grateful for the practice that when a novice had a feast day she was seated next to Mother Gertrude. I prayed for an early Sister's feast day. Unfortunately, my feast day fell just two weeks after I was moved! Back to square one.

The day after I came out of my Canonical year, I was summoned to Mother Gertrude's office and informed that Sister Martina was sick and that I was to replace her as the fifth and sixth grade teacher at Cathedral Presentation Elementary School in San Francisco.

My heart sank. There were other Sisters senior to me who should have been assigned the position. I hated leaving the security of the novitiate and sent off to a mission. It was required that I wear a black veil so it didn't appear that I was a novice. I was nineteen years old and had no experience as a teacher. I would change into my black veil and meet Sisters Paula Marie (principal), Vibianna and Helen at the front door to drive to school. Every morning, I would rush into the guest bathroom on the first floor and get sick to my stomach. Once I got to school, I was fine. I enjoyed the children and the challenge of teaching them.

I prayed each day that Sister Martina would get well and I wouldn't have to leave the novitiate. It was a safe haven. However my prayers were not answered. Sister Martina died and I spent the next three years teaching at Cathedral Presentation.

When the second year of my Novitiate came to an end, it was voted that I would be professed. I was delighted to be professed and officially receive the black veil but knew I would miss the novitiate.

7

My Junior Years

There are three celebrations that occur during our early Religious life. The day we receive the habit, the day we are Professed and the day that we take our final vows and receive the ring.

On December 23rd, I once again processed into the chapel to receive my black veil and take temporary vows of Obedience, Poverty and Celibacy for three years. First Profession was open to family members so my mother, father, and Kay were once again seated in the front row while Casey served in the sanctuary.

Kay later pumped Casey to tell her what he saw when they removed my white veil and clothed me in the black veil. Much to her disappointment, he said the change was so fast that he saw nothing. If he had, he would have seen a bald head topped with a little white cap. I had shaved my head for purposes of hygiene since our heads were covered around the clock. We even wore a night veil to bed.

Having received the black veil, I knew it was only a matter of time until I would be moved downstairs with the other Sisters and become a member of the Professed community. It was a sad day when Sisters Cornelia, Honora and myself left the novitiate.

Sister Cornelia and I went out each morning to teach at Cathedral Presentation. It was comforting to have a novitiate companion with me. Our drive to and from school was quite an experience. Sister Vibiana, who was only one of two licensed drivers in the Congregation, transported us to school. She must have been in her eighties. Upon driving over a curb she would exclaim, "Someone must have moved the curb." Another time, we had to pull into a gas station because smoke was pouring out from under the hood. The gas station attendant called to us to get out of the car lest it burn into flames. Gratefully, when Sister Vibiana became ill they took the car keys from her.

True to the promise I had made years earlier, I told my students that they may ask me any question and I would answer them. A hand went up immediately and Anthony asked, "Sister, John the Baptist was born without Original Sin and

Mary was conceived without Original Sin. What is the difference?" I blushed at the thought of explaining the difference. Thankfully, I was saved by the recess bell. "Anthony, I will answer your question after recess," I replied. The gods were shining down on me. Anthony didn't bother to repeat the question when we came in from recess.

Another promise I made would allow the children to draw whatever they wished and I would help them. Anthony decided to draw a picture of Jesus. When I came to him, he was having trouble so I began to erase, redraw, and erase again. When all that was left was a hole in the paper, I said to Anthony, "We should try something less difficult, like a landscape." I was good at landscapes.

Another memory that lingers from this time that I taught at Cathedral Presentation has to do with a boy named Harold. Harold arrived one day with a science project and asked if he could show it to the class. I told him that we would view it at the end of the day. The bell for dismissal rang and there was no time for Harold's presentation.

I later regretted not letting Harold show his project when I learned that he was living with a stepfather that treated him badly. Things got to be so bad that Harold stole his stepfather's motorcycle and drove it across the bay bridge just to get away. School for Harold was a haven where he felt safe. The Monday morning after Harold took off, he came to school and as the children lined up to come into the building, I noticed that his face and hands were dirty. I told Harold to go to the boy's bathroom and clean up. It was located in the basement of the school.

We no sooner came into the building when I saw two policemen at the door. Having sent the children to their respective classes, I opened the door to the officers.

"Sister, we are looking for Harold. Is he here?"

"Officers, I will let you know when and if Harold comes to school," I replied. All the while I was praying that Harold would not appear, back from the bathroom.

After school, I walked Harold home. He lived just up the block from the school in an apartment building.

"Sister, my stepfather is going to kill me," he said to me.

"Harold, I assure you that nothing is going to happen to you." We took the elevator up to the second floor, approached the door to his apartment, and rang the bell. A lovely lady opened the door and reached out to hug Harold.

"Harold, you had me worried to death," she exclaimed. I related the episode with the police and she thanked me profusely for not handing Harold over to them.

"Sister, my husband is very hard on Harold and I have told him time and again that he is too demanding. I will speak to him again and make it clear that if he doesn't soften his ways with Harold, I will leave him."

She must have succeeded in getting through to her husband because Harold seemed so much happier and there was never a repeat incident on Harold's part.

The most traumatic experience I had at Cathedral occurred when we had a terrific storm and the bay window in the front office blew in, letting the rain pour inside. The principal had been absent for weeks with a sprained ankle and I was in charge while teaching the fifth, sixth, seventh, and eighth grade classes at the same time. I grabbed the phone and crawled under the desk to call my superior to tell her I would be late. She couldn't seem to understand that I had to wait for the window man before leaving. It was at this point I wished I had joined the Carmelites—a cloistered community that spent their days in prayer.

One day I came home to the Mother House, to be told that my personal effects had been moved to Saint Agnes, where I would reside. My mind quickly flashed back to the condition I had left my cell in that morning. Hopefully no stockings hanging on the towel rack!

Later, I was assigned to Saint Anne's while still teaching at Cathedral and I found myself praying for the day when I would teach at a school where I lived. The dinner conversation was always all about what happened at school that day and I had little to contribute. It was during that time that I first heard the many stories of Danny Walsh who is now the bishop of Santa Rosa.

Saint Anne's proved to be a trial period in my life. I was constantly called to the Superior's office to be reprimanded for something I had done. One time it was because I didn't tell two sisters who were talking in the Solarium that they shouldn't be talking. Another time I was taken to the refectory and shown some black marks on the wall above the server's table. I had to get a ladder to wash them off! The final straw came one Saturday morning when, once again, I was summoned to the Superior's office. This time I was shown two check aprons that had Clorox stains on them. My charge was to clean the laundry room, not to do the wash. After kneeling and listening to the accusation by the Superior, I stood up and told her, "If you ever accuse me again of something that I haven't done, I will walk out of this office, down the stairs and out the front door. I will then take the street car to the Mother House and tell Mother Olivia that I have had it!" She never accused me again.

Finally, my dream of living in a convent adjacent to the school was granted! It was the summer of 1951 and I was living at the Mother House while attending the University of San Francisco. I was serving in the refectory when Mother

Olivia said that she wanted to see me after the meal. I was so busy serving that I didn't hear when she told the sisters that we were opening a new school in San Lorenzo. The other sisters made the connection and called out to me.

"Did you hear what Mother Olivia said Cahterine Laboure? We think you are going to San Lorenzo!" Their prediction was accurate. Mother Olivia informed me that I was going to San Lorenzo with Sisters Mary Consolata and Edward Joseph.

We opened the new school in October of 1951 and moved into a house built during the time of the Civil War. It was the time of the "baby boom" and far more applications poured in than we could accommodate. I remember the pastor, Father Dermody, went over the applications with us and I smiled at his selections. He made sure that there was a doctor, dentist, plumber and electrician's child represented.

Sister Consolata had only taught the eighth grade so she took the third grade, and I had only taught fifth and sixth graders so I was given the second grade. Edward Joseph would teach the first grade. The year and a half that I spent at St. John the Baptist were among my happiest.

Edward Joseph had a great sense of humor and it carried us through the many challenges of opening a new school. Many nights we didn't eat dinner until 9:00 p.m. Since neither Edward Joseph nor I were cooks, we decided that we would cook each dinner together. I'll never forget when we attempted our first venture in cooking a Thanksgiving turkey. Thinking that if we stuffed the bird from the tail it would go out the other end, we sewed up the neck area. No matter how hard we pushed, we couldn't get the stuffing to fill the neck cavity, so we cut the strings and proceeded to fill the neck cavity. Not knowing how long to roast the turkey, we didn't put it into the oven until around noon. The turkey weighed 20 lbs.! Sister Consolata invited Sister Monina and Attracta for Thanksgiving dinner, which was to be served at 3:00 p.m.

Sister Edward Joseph's brother had given us money to buy a small bottle of brandy to light the plum pudding, so we crossed Lewelling Bulevard and headed for the market. When we arrived home, I tripped and the brandy bottle landed on the steps and broke into pieces. Back to the store we went, only to hear the clerk remark, "Sisters, you really went through that brandy quickly!"

One of our first obstacles came when I couldn't get the washing machine to work. I called the company and they sent out a man to correct the problem. Much to my embarrassment he said, "Sister, it helps if you plug it in." He then went on to say that we could even dye in our machine. With that, Edward Joseph and I burst into laughter. By this time, after all of the demands that came with opening a school and a convent, we were ready to crawl in and to die.

As the dedication for the new school drew near, there was even more work to be done. Knowing that all of the sisters would come, we had to figure out how we could accommodate them for refreshments. It was decided that Edward Joseph and I would paint the room in the attic and pick up unfinished chairs, which we would stain. Apart from putting the convent in order, we had to prepare the school for its many visitors. This entailed decorating the classrooms and displaying the children's work. If we got to bed by midnight during those days it was a wonder.

The day finally arrived. Standing at the door of the convent, the Archbishop greeted each of the sisters as she arrived. The line seemed endless and it was told that at one point he was heard to say, "Are the sisters coming around a second time?"

One of the most touching memories I have from that year occurred on the last day of school when all of the children had been dismissed. Peter Desmond remained behind and offered to clean the erasers and empty the waste paper basket. When he finished and was on his way out, he stopped, gave me a hug and said, "Sister, I love you and I will always love you." Tears sprang up in my eyes as I responded, "Peter, I too love you."

In January of my second year at St. John The Baptist, I came down with pneumonia. Due to the scar tissue from my previous bouts with pneumonia, the doctor advised my superior to have me moved to a drier climate. It was decided that I should move to Los Angeles. Amid copious tears, I boarded the train for Los Angeles and Our Lady of Loretto grammar school. My friend, Sister Evangelist (Joann O'Shea) was to be my replacement, while I, in turn, would take her fourth grade class.

8

My Final Professed Years

I arrived in Los Angeles and was met by Sister Mary Cleta (The Superior) and Sister Mary Baptist. It was my first trip to Los Angeles. Having been assigned to the fourth grade, I visited the classroom and was grateful that Sister Mary Evangelist had decorated the room. The first morning that I crossed the schoolyard, I heard one child say to another, "Isn't she beautiful!" What a nice first encounter with the students.

After the first year, I was assigned to teach a fifth and sixth grade class. Since this was a new combination of two grades, an unused classroom was set up to accommodate the class. Sister Baptist and I had the task of readying the room, which showed its lack of use for years. Cobwebs everywhere, desks covered with dust and a floor that needed washing and waxing. The day we took on the cleanup, it was a 105 degrees! You can imagine our plight, clothed in 5 yards of surge and a headgear that covered all but our faces mopping, scrubbing and dusting. We had to be careful while cleaning around the platform, which held the teacher's desk, because the floorboards were tenuous. Later I would have to remind the children not to come up to my desk because the floor wouldn't hold them.

Many of the students needed remedial work because they had difficulty with the curriculum and some had learning disabilities. I remember when I called on Peter Distaso to read, the children called out, "Sister, Peter can't read." They were right.

I asked Peter to stay back when class was over and said, "Peter, I am going to go over two paragraphs from the Catholic Messenger with you that I want you to read tomorrow." With my help, he memorized the paragraphs. The next day I called on Peter to read. Without any hesitation and much to the amazement of his classmates, he read the two paragraphs. From that day forward, Peter read. He had merely been made to believe that he couldn't read.

Roger, another student of mine, simply could not learn to add. Every effort on my part failed. Years later I learned that he owned his own store and used an adding machine.

Bob Lodolo was an endless source of entertainment. He had a dry wit, which never failed to make me laugh. His mother, Bianca, was the first woman to do yard duty. The Lodolos lived across the driveway from the convent. I must admit that Bob was and is my favorite student. Both he and his beautiful wife, Barbara, came to my Golden Jubilee a few years back and I was delighted that he hadn't lost his dry sense of humor. He would relish telling the story that his older sister would tell him that he was adopted and that his parents were going to come and get him and take him away! His sister is now Sister Lucia.

It was a sad day for me when the Lodolo family moved. I missed Bob.

I came to love this class. Because I had difficulty for my first six years of schooling, I made sure that I would never make a demand of a student that would embarrass them. I made sure that I would give a positive response even when I was given a wrong answer. We got along so well.

The second year ended and I was heartbroken to learn that I was being transferred to Holy Trinity School in San Pedro. I felt that I was needed at Loretto. However, my stay at Holy Trinity would be a turning point in my life.

Sister Joan Murphy had been appointed Superior at Holy Trinity. I was so taken by the fact that she took time to meet with every sister assigned to Holy Trinity. I was in bed at the time she came to see me. I had just come home from the hospital where I had my tonsils removed. They were badly infected and I was required to stay in bed for a time. I hid the directions for follow up after the operation so that I could go to Lake Arrowhead for vacation. Unfortunately, a sister who was a nurse asked for the follow up directions. I never made it to Arrowhead.

Joan was so kind and warm that I loved her from the beginning! I remember on Retreat Sunday she gave us a beautiful talk and met with each one of us. Sister Robert (Mary Jane Floyd) met me on the stairs and said, "If we don't become saints after that, we never will!"

The community was made up of young sisters who got along, and we all prayed that we wouldn't get a call saying that we were changed. The reason being that every house had to have a sister who could play the organ (Joan could play) and a sister to drive. None of us drove. Thankfully, Sister Mary Raymond learned to drive.

At the time we were not to watch television unless it was educational. Joan believed that Perry Mason taught logical thinking and Lawrence Welk provided music appreciation. Every Saturday night we watched both programs.

I spent a good deal of time meditating on the Chapter of Obedience in our Constitution. Sister Joan would send me to the chapel after I had disobeyed an order. One time I was sick, but got up and dressed anyway. I was tired of being in bed.

It was while I was in San Pedro that my mother died. I was devastated. I always prayed that I would die before my mother. She was just 56 yrs old. It was a heart attack. Joan was so solicitous and understanding. Traveling home, it was my first plane trip. The man sitting next to me kept reaching over to look out the window. I gladly exchanged seats with him.

Mother was waked in San Jose and buried in the Jesuit cemetery at Santa Clara. Dad was close to a Jesuit priest, Father Ziemann, and had helped him with financial matters. In gratitude, it was arranged that both mother and dad would be buried there. It was a practice at the time that you either attended the rosary or the funeral. I chose the funeral but promised that, if I ever became a superior, sisters would attend both! Sisters did not attend the funeral of a sister's family member. I would see to it that every sister in the community would attend the funeral. Sister Doreen Healy was an exception. She came to the funeral.

I was given the seventh grade at Holy Trinity and it was the age of baby boomers. Seventy-five children were in my class. There were so many children that the teacher's desk was placed in the corridor! After the fire in Chicago, where many students died, a law was passed where you could only have 50 students in a class. The pastor enrolled 55 believing that some would drop out. Rarely was that the case. Thankfully my desk was placed back into the classroom.

Since I was vice principal, when Joan was away, I was in charge. It never failed that there would be a crisis. One morning a lady who was expecting a baby brought her children to school. The contractions began to occur, and she laid down on the couch in the nurses room. I prayed, "Dear God, don't let her have her baby now!" The contractions slowed and her husband came and took her to the hospital. Another time the fire inspector came to observe a fire drill. I rang the alarm but had no idea where the key was to turn it off. I asked Dennis to please hold his finger on the button until the officer left hoping that the chief wouldn't spot Dennis in the building during the drill. With a great deal of tape, I was able to turn the alarm off. Joan showed me where the key was and that relieved future anxiety.

The Major Superior came on her yearly visitation and when she left, I found Joan in tears. "What happened?" I asked. She told me that she had been reprimanded for a number of things. One being that she insisted that the Sisters eat an egg every day. Some Sister had obviously reported this. What the other issues were, I don't remember. I just remember that I was furious! The next day I wrote the Major Superior that I wanted an appointment when I came to San Francisco in June. The Major Superior was the same Superior that I had at St. Anne's.

I mentioned to one of the Sisters that I intended to confront the Major Superior. She couldn't believe it. However, she said, "I admire your courage. I could never bring myself to do that."

The day arrived for my meeting with the Major Superior. With butterflies in my stomach, I knocked on her door and entered, kneeling at her feet. I proceeded to share with her my anger for what she put Joan through. I have no recollection of what followed, but I felt better for having confronted her.

That summer I was enrolled in a program at Holy Cross in Oregon. Sisters tried to tell me that it was a program for Superiors and I must be going to become a Superior. I didn't believe them. However, I soon found out that it was indeed a program for Superiors!

On my return, Joan and I were summoned to the Major Superior's office. Joan went first and I was to follow after lunch. I noticed that Joan was crying and I was furious. If she had been reprimanded again, I would blow my top!

After lunch I waited outside the office door until a buzzer invited me in to meet the Major Superior. Kneeling at her feet, she handed me an envelope. It was my assignment to be the Superior at St. Mary Magdalene!

9

My Years as a Superior

In August of 1959, I was on vacation at Presentation Center when I was told that our Major Superior wished to see me. Sisters Joan Murphy and Kathleen Griffen were likewise summoned to meet with the Major Superior. As we made our way to the Mother House we discussed what the reason for the summons could be.

When we arrived at the Mother House, Sister Joan went in first to meet with the Major Superior. Kathleen and I waited in the chapel. I needed to prepare myself for what was to come! Since Joan was still with the Superior, I left the chapel and headed for the refectory and lunch. When I entered the refectory and bowed to the crucifix, which was our custom, I saw that Joan was seated next to the superior at the head table and it looked as if she had been crying. My first thought was that she had been reprimanded for something and I felt real anger at this!

When we exited the refectory I proceeded up the stairs to the Superior's office and waited for the buzzer, which indicated that I was to enter. I felt my heart pounding as I knelt before the superior and she handed me an envelope. With trembling hands I opened it and read the contents. It informed me that I was appointed superior of Saint Mary Magdalene in Los Angeles! Given the number of times that I had confronted her, I couldn't believe that she would appoint me a Superior! I was twenty-nine years old, which meant that I would be the youngest Superior.

Saint Mary Magdalene was a large community, housing thirteen Sisters. I would later find out that most of the Sisters were much older than I. Five of them were old enough to be my mother and two old enough to be my grandmother! Three of the Sisters had been my teachers in high school. Only three would be younger than me.

To add to my concern, I was not to be the principal, but would teach the seventh grade. I was surprised that I had the presence of mind to ask, "Mother, where is the line drawn between the principal and the superior in terms of authority?"

She replied, "We will discuss that later." Later never came!

My concern rested on the fact that the principal had a reputation for being stern. In fact when the Sisters heard that she was being transferred, they were delighted. Their delight didn't last long. Sister's assignment had been changed and she would stay as the principal!

I was touched that Mother had told Joan that I wouldn't be returning to Holy Trinity, knowing how hard it would be on both of us. Joan always said that I had taught her to love. I cried copious tears because I would so miss Joan as well as the Sisters and the parishioners, including the children that I had taught.

After our vacation, Joan went on retreat in Berkeley, and I went back to Holy Trinity to pack. Sister Hubert, a junior professed Sister, accompanied me to San Pedro. She was a driver and could transport me between St. Mary Magdalene and Holy Trinity. Every night, I would call Joan and cry over the phone! When Hubert and I were moving my things out of San Pedro, I would separate myself so that she didn't see my tears!

Finally all of my belongings were at St. Mary Magdalene's and I moved in. I'll never forget opening the side door of the convent and seeing Sister Martha, who was old enough to be my grandmother, on her hands and knees waxing the corridor floor!. I felt so humble and said, "Sister, I don't want you waxing the floor. I will finish it."

She said, "You can't, you're the superior!"

"That is why I can," I replied.

Sister Regina, the former superior, had moved out of her room so that I could move in. Again, I felt so humble and told her it was not necessary to move out of her room. I would move in after she left. However, she wouldn't hear of it. It was brought home to me how much we reverence our superiors regardless of age.

Sister Mary Daniel and Mary Doris were appointed councilors. I would become a close friend of Sister Daniel and that friendship has lasted for more than forty years.

I was heart broken when Sister Daniel was later appointed Superior of Saint Agnes in San Francisco, which meant she would be moving. I so missed her. It's the price we pay when we allow ourselves to become vulnerable! I called her frequently and so looked forward to Superior Meetings when I could spend time with her and with Joan.

Whenever I was assigned a convent to stay during these meetings, it was never Saint Agnes! The aversion to "particular friendships" was still in vogue! I firmly believe that the love of God and fellowship with Christ comes through friendship. It has been my experience that whenever I was assigned to a new mission, I discovered a friend. The price you pay is the deep hurt that comes from separation, be it distance or death.

My first action was to meet with them in a front parlor and make clear that they shared my responsibility to form community. My second action was to assemble the Sisters and explain that I was making changes to some of our practices. I told them that they were to seal, stamp and put their mail out to be sent. It was a practice that Sisters left their letter unsealed on the Superior's desk. I then informed them that they did not have to ask permission to turn on the television. I just asked that they be sensitive to the Sisters working in the community room.

I used to dread it when a Sister came into my office, knelt down, kissed the floor and accused herself of something she had done and wished to make a reparation for it. Many times it was because she broke a dish or a glass. So many of the accusations were about an accident, not anything deliberate. I made it clear to the Sisters that when they had an accident, it was not necessary to make a reparation. However, if in anger they threw a dish at a Sister, that would be a different story. The Sisters laughed at that. Gratefully, it was rare that a Sister came to me to make a reparation!

I then informed them that I was leaving a box at the foot of the Blessed Mother with $75.00 in petty cash. If they felt they needed money when they went out, they were to take what they needed and note it in the notebook next to the box. It had been a practice that a Sister needed to ask for the money she might need when she went out. A Superior could just take what she needed. So often we had to meet a Sister at the airport and more often than not the flight was delayed. Sometimes the wait was long enough that you would like to have lunch, or buy a book. Why should it be different for the Sisters? The Sisters only had a dime to make a telephone call in an emergency.

Given this disparity between a Sister and a superior, I believed that it was a double standard. I'll never forget the first Superior's meeting when I raised my hand to be acknowledged by the Major Superior. We were sitting in a horseshoe arrangement facing the Major Superior's table. "Yes, Sister what do you have to say?" she asked.

I responded, "I think we have a double standard." Every veiled head turned to me! You would have thought that I suggested blowing up the Mother House!

"And Sister, why do you think that?"

"Well," I said, "Two weeks ago when I was made a Superior, I could take whatever money I thought I needed when going out. Before that time I had a dime to make a phone call in an emergency. I believe this is a double standard."

"And what do you suggest, Sister?" I then told them how I place a petty cash box at the end of the corridor, which is available to the Sisters. Within a month every house had a petty cash box. I also pointed out that as a Superior I could mail my own letters. I told the Sisters that I was leaving stamps out and to please seal their letters, stamp them and put them out to be mailed. Again, within a month, the direction went out stating that Sisters seal their own letters and put them out to be mailed.

As mature women, I felt that the Sisters should be free to turn on the television without asking permission. That too was sent out as a directive.

At the same meeting was a Franciscan Priest who was asked to address the Superiors. His topic included the wearing of the habit. I asked him, "Father, do you wear your habit when you are on vacation?"

"No, Sister," was his response. I then went on to say that we should have the same option to dispense with the habit and wear secular close. It is embarrassing to go to the beach in full habit. So many cartoons illustrated Sisters playing in the water while in full habit. When we go out in public, we are easily recognized as Sisters. There are times when you go out to dinner and do not wish to be noticed. After much discussion, it was decided that Sisters could choose to wear secular clothes when on vacation, or when they did not wish to be identified as a Nun for the sake of privacy. Given the option to wear secular clothes, we were forced to grow our hair and to style it. One benefit for me in wearing the habit was that I didn't have to worry about my hair!

It was while I was at the Mother House that I was instructed by my doctor to divest myself of the bandeau (Head Band) because it was eventually going to cause cancer given its pressure on my forehead. When I went home I approached Mother Thadea, who was the Assistant to the Mother General, and told her that I couldn't wear the habit without the headgear. It would look ridiculous. I was given permission to purchase a black suit, which meant that my legs would be exposed. An elderly Sister, Sister Martha, followed me around and said that I was a source of temptation. I took it as a compliment. Gratefully, one of the young Sisters came to my cell and styled my hair each morning. I can still remember the butterflies that I had in my stomach the first morning that I walked into the chapel without my habit, before the gazes of all of the Sisters.

My years as a Superior brought their challenges. The first year, three Sisters had hysterectomies and I finally asked the doctor if they were contagious! Sister

Basil arrived at St. Mary Magdalene my second year and I noticed that she did not genuflect when she passed the chapel. Later I asked her why. She responded, "I have bad knees and find it hard to bend them." This didn't seem right so I made an appointment with an orthopedic doctor to examine Sister. Doctor Sing informed Sister in my presence that she needed to have knee surgery before her condition worsened. I called the Mother House and informed the Major Superior that Basil needed surgery. She agreed to it. The morning of the surgery the Major Superior was there and as they rolled Sister Basil into surgery, she turned and said to me, "If anything goes wrong, you are responsible, since you chose the doctor."

"Dear God, don't let anything go wrong!" I prayed.

We only had one car which the Sisters used to go to Conaty High School to teach every day. I needed a car to visit Basil so I asked the pastor if I could use his car, which he no longer drove. It was just sitting in the garage. He agreed and gave me the keys. However during the time he was in Ireland, he wanted to store the car with friends. So when I went to give him the keys, I told him that I would have to call a cab to visit Sister Basil in the hospital and it would be charged to the parish! He literally threw the keys across the desk to me and said, "You are a difficult nun! Take the car."

It didn't take long before it became evident that the principal, Sister Berchmans and I did not see eye to eye on many occasions. Sisters Anthony Daniel and Hubert had never taught before and it was helpful to them to have worksheets for their students. However, the principal would only give them one master carbon for the week! I bought a box of carbons and left them in the workroom. It didn't go over well with the principal!

One day it was pouring rain and Sister Berchmans did not want the children to come into the building until the bell rang. I informed her that I did not want the Sisters standing out in the rain supervising the children for fear that they would catch cold. This must have been the proverbial straw that broke the camel's back because Sister called the Mother House and complained to the Mother General about me.

Soon after, Sister Ann Cecily informed me that the Mother General and her assistant needed to be picked up at the airport. They would be staying at the convent. I couldn't figure out why she was coming since it wasn't time for the annual visitation.

Once Mother got settled, she called me to her room. I knelt down at her feet, a practice that I did not agree with. She quickly made it known to me why she came. The principal had called her and reported me. She began to list the complaints that she had received. I didn't reprimand the Sisters when they talked and laughed in the corridor. I was always calling for a party. The Sisters were allowed to turn the television on whenever they wished. Further more, I was using scotch tape to hang pictures in my classroom which took the paint off the walls! The list went on and on. I finally had it! I stood up and headed for the door, telling her that she could appoint another Superior to take my place. I no longer wished to be the Superior. As far as I was concerned, she could appoint the principal Superior!

I no sooner put my hand on the door knob when she called, "Sister Catherine Laboure' come back here!" I didn't kneel this time but stood up in front of her as she went on to say that we both knew that Sister had a problem and that she doubted I was guilty of the things Sister reported about me.

Gratefully, the next year I was appointed principal and did not have to deal with a principal whose values were contrary to mine. Sister Berchmans was sent to another school. Since I was both principal and Superior, I did not have to teach a class. However, that didn't last long. I had arranged for the community to take a trip to the snow and while there, Sister Roberta twisted her leg while coming down on a sled. She thought if she walked up and down it would get better. Not so! She only made it wors and ended up having surgery. My seventh grade teacher, Sister Ann Cecily was sent to replace her and I inherited the seventh grade!

I came up with a marvelous idea of how we could bring all of the Sisters in Los Angeles together for a fun day. It was a custom to have the Sisters come together once a year, but I soon learned that some of the Sisters complained of a headache and asked not to go. I came to the realization that they were nervous about meeting all of the Sisters, wondering who they would talk to, and who would talk to them. I thought if we had a carnival day with games, prizes and a movie, Sisters would look forward to coming. My friend Kay Hamilton secured a cotton candy, a snow cone and a popcorn machine as well as carnival games. I rounded up great prizes and Sister Helena arranged them in a display in the front parlor. I rented "The Court Jester" with Danny Kaye, knowing that it would be hilarious. Everyone was given play money to spend on the games and treats. We made up box lunches. Soft drinks were placed in an ice chest for the taking. The day proved a huge success and not a single Sister stayed away. They expressed the hope that we would do it again next year. But I was informed that I was not to do it again. One of the Sisters reported to the Mother General that we shouldn't do this in Los Angeles because it wasn't done in San Francisco. I said, let San Francisco have a similar event. However, the suggestion didn't go over, and I was not allowed to host another event.

Monsinor Morris, the pastor, moved to Ireland permanently and Monsigno Clyne, the Superintendent of Schools, was assigned to Saint Mary Magdalene's parish. He arrived in May just before we had our annual "play day" to raise money for the teacher's salaries during the summer. Tickets were sold for lunch, games and a raffle. The festivities started at lunch time. When the pastor heard of it, he told me that it wouldn't look good if the Superintendent allowed for a half day off school for his parish school. I told him that's fine but then he would have to pay the salaries of the teachers during the summer. He said, "I'll just be away that day and say I wasn't aware of what was going on at the school!" Money works wonders!

I had the checkbook for the school and the pastor asked to see it. He hadn't returned it to me when it came time for me to pay the taxes. When I called him, he said it was at the chancery office. I said, "Fine, I'll call the chancery office and let them know that I need the check book." He slammed the phone down! The checkbook was in the convent mailbox within the hour. It seemed like I was destined to confront authority at every turn.

A Chapter of Elections was held in June of 1962, and I was a delegate to the Chapter since there were thirteen Sisters in the house, which constituted that the Superior would be a delegate. My prayer was that Joan would be elected. I had no idea that many Sisters were thinking the same. Sister Robert, my friend from San Pedro, was a delegate and I knew she would have the same hope that I did that Joan would be elected.

The Chapter was held at the Mother House and, because the room was so close to the other parts of the Mother House, we wore ear phones and an electric board was placed on our desk which was used for voting. You pressed a green light for yes and a red light for no. You were forced to concentrate to make sure you pushed the right button. Sister Annunciata who was sitting next to me, would ask each time, "What button do I push for yes?" It made me wonder how many wrong votes registered.

When it came time to elect the Major Superior, you were given white beans (yes) and black beans (no), which you dropped in the basket and dropped, indicating if you were voting for the nominated Sister. It eventually came down to two names, the incumbent Superior and Joan. We then went into the chapel with small white pieces of paper to write the name of our choice to be placed in the basket. There was a representative from the hierarchy present to assure that the elections were legitimate. There was no chance of stuffing the ballot box. Apart from the representative, two tellers were elected to count the votes and make sure they matched the number of the delegates. Electing the tellers was the first business of the chapter. I remember that one delegated nominated a Sister who had been dead for two years. It caused me concern regarding the eligibility of at least one delegate!

Each of us took our place in the chapel with pencil and paper in hand. I wrote Joan's name and made my way up to the altar to drop my ballot into the box. When everyone had voted, the teller called the name out. The first ballot was close, and neither had a majority. Two more ballots were taken and still no majority. The third ballot would be decided by who had the most votes. I kept looking at my ballot to make sure that I had written Joan's name. I could feel the perspiration running down my body. Joan won by one vote! I had to dispose of my habit since I couldn't get rid of the perspiration odor.

After the outcome, I went to the cell that I shared with Sister Miriam Joseph and found her jumping up and down on the bed shouting, "We have elected a John XXIII!" She was referring to Pope John XXIII who shortly after election called for a Vatican II Council at which all of the bishops in the world would gather in Rome to update the Church. It had been one hundred years since Vatican I. It was later discovered that John XXIII was elected because the cardinals thought he was too old to do anything significant!

Since Vatican II (1963-1964), the Church has never been the same. It was later said of the Council that, "The windows and doors of the Church have been opened!"

Joan's election would do the same for our Congregation. She was a prophet! The tension was so great after the election that Joan called for a recess until the next day. One Sister accused me of campaigning for Joan. I told her that I had no contact with the Sisters in the Bay Area and spent no time talking to the Sisters in Los Angeles about my hopes that Joan would be elected.

Shortly after her election, Joan called me and told me that she was going to send the Sisters preparing for final profession to Saint Mary Magdalene for their remote retreat. I was to give them a lecture twice a day and she wanted me to tape the lectures. Soon after, Joan called me and said that one of the Sisters told her that if she sent the young Sisters to Los Angeles, they would all leave. My response was, "Joan, better they leave now than later!" Not only did they all stay, but one of the Sisters who wanted to make the retreat but did not wish to be finally professed asked to make final profession after the retreat!

I was delighted to give the retreat because it meant that I could order books to prepare my lectures and I would be doing what I loved to do—read! Without a doubt I bought every book on theology and Scripture that had been published in the last two years. Sister Anthony Daniel, who did my laundry and turned my bed down each night, had the task of moving the open books on the bed to the floor and then replacing them back on the bed every day. I even had an open book by the tub in the bathroom!

Knowing that I would have to get away for a day each week during the retreat, I asked Marlene, our P.E. teacher if she would teach me how to drive. I had avoided learning to drive because I felt that I would be lost in thought and go through a red light or stop sign. I remember I had something on my mind while I was crossing the street to mail a letter and a car came to a screeching halt and my cincture was caught on the bumper! My companion said, Catherine Laboure', you could have been hit, you need to think what you are doing!"

Marlene was an excellent teacher. She had me parallel parking with in no time. When I went to take my driving lesson the instructor asked if I had driven a cab! I smile when I remember as we drove out of the parking lot to go home, Marlene said, "Do you know what you just did, Sister? You went through a red light!" I vowed to concentrate on my driving in the future. Thankfully, I have a perfect driving record today so I must have kept my vow.

When Joan had asked me to conduct the remote retreat for the Sisters, she told me that I should talk to Father Bro who was into using films to teach theology and spirituality. He gave me a book on the subject as well as suggestions on how to recognize the implications of the film in terms of theology. As an example, he spoke of the film, "A Street Car Named Desire," and showed how it was a story of Conversion.

The summer that the Sisters arrived, Immaculate Heart College was showing a film every Friday night, which was open to the public. I was delighted to find out that the first film was, "A Street Car Named Desire." The Sisters and I would go every Friday night to Immaculate Heart College to see the film. The next day we would discuss the film in terms of theology. I was also given tickets for the film, "Dr. Zhivago," which was a classic. It made our discussions both relevant and entertaining. Joan received flak from a few Sisters who were greatly disturbed that I was taking the Junior Professed Sisters to the movies! Joan informed them that she had approved of it. Criticism never forced Joan to change her mind if she felt it was not right.

The Sisters told me later that it was the best summer that they had ever had. I was so touched when, on the day before we were to go to the Mother House, they had me go down stairs to the basement where they had made decorations for every month of the school year! They worked on them when I took off on Fridays.

It was during this summer that Pope Paul VI sent out an order that all Religious Congregations were to modify their habits. Our habit consisted of five yards of serge, which meant we kept the sidewalks swept as we walked along! The headgear was to be modified so that Sisters had peripheral vision, and not have a veil that prevented full vision. I had the added responsibility of arranging for the Junior Sisters to alter their head gear before they returned to the Mother House for Final Profession. Thankfully, we had a seamstress in the parish who came and helped the Sisters in the sewing of the veil.

On December 7, 1963, Joan called me and said that my Father had an accident and burned himself. I was to book the earliest flight, and she and Cleta would meet the plane. I thought maybe he burned his foot or some other part of his body. When I arrived at the hospital, I learned that ninety eight percent of his body had been burned. His nylon robe had caught fire on the wall heater. When I went in to see him, I focused on his eyes. Only his face escaped the flames. When I approached the bed, he asked, "Jane, can you get me a cigarette?"

"Daddy," I said, "You can't have one until the doctors and nurses finish removing the burnt skin."

There were nine doctors and nurses working on him. He felt no pain because all of his nerve endings were burnt. I prayed that God would take him. Kay joined me we went back to the Mother House to stay overnight. We stayed in the guest room, which had electric blankets. In a fit of distraught laughter we said, "Wouldn't it be something if we went up in flames!"

My brother, Casey, flew down from Los Angeles and stayed overnight with Pat, our cousin who was very close to Casey. Since it was late, they would come to the hospital the next morning. They tell the story that the two of them were crying when the doorbell rang and it was a salesman selling vacuum cleaners. When he saw the two of them he said, "Don't feel bad. A lot of people don't buy from me!"

When Kay and I arrived at the hospital early the next morning, we were informed that dad had died. As heartbroken as we were, we thanked God that he took him. I didn't know how I could bear to see him in that state. Gratefully, Casey didn't have to see his burnt body. He could remember dad as he was before the accident. Joan, as thoughtful as always, had me stay with Sister Daniel at St. Agnes until after the funeral. So, unlike my Mother's funeral, all the Sisters were present for the rosary, and those not teaching attended the funeral.

It came time for me to fly back to Los Angeles and I knew that I had to be in good spirits for the Sisters since we would be getting ready for Christmas. As Superior, I would make sure the Sisters had presents on Christmas Day. I remember driving to the airport in the evening and seeing all of the Christmas lights and glowing decorations. I couldn't understand how people could be celebrating Christmas when my Father had died!

It wasn't long after that Joan came to St Mary Magdalene to inform me that she was appointing me Misstress of Juniors and I would be moving to the Mother House. No amount of persuasion succeeded in changing her mind. However, Joan was thoughtful as usual. She had Sister Daniel come down and help me move. Kay Hamilton had given me a used car. While we were driving to San Francisco, the hood kept popping open. It made for a challenging move!

10

Mistress of Junior Sisters

The afternoon that Sister Daniel and I arrived in San Francisco was clear and sunny. Not at all like my mood. I was already missing Saint Mary Magdalene and dreading my appointment as Mistress of Junior Sisters.

Daniel helped me to move in and get settled while I tried to hold back the tears. My bedroom and office were located at the far end of the second corridor. The window overlooked the fire escape with a red light over my door declaring, "EXIT." I later told said to Joan, "Either the red light has to go or my title—'Mistress'!" My title was quickly changed to Director of Junior Sisters.

The Junior Sisters were not to arrive for another day or two. Joan, hoping to cheer me up, took Sister Mary of the Trinity, Clare and I to see "A Thousand and One Clowns" with Jason Robard. I laughed so hard that the usher came down the aisle and signaled me with his flashlight to keep it down. It was great therapy for me.

One of the requests that I made of Joan was that I would have my own checking account. She agreed, and had three hundred dollars deposited into a "Library" account for me every month. I had also brought my own money with me, knowing that I would want to treat the Sisters on occasion and order books for the House. I knew I would be able to draw content for my talks from the books.

It was difficult for Joan to go into the community room and enjoy a T.V. program without a Sister coming to her with a problem. So one Saturday I went to Sears and bought a small, black and white television for her room. Not wanting any Sisters to see me carrying a T.V., I hid it under my large sleeves. That night, Trin, Clare, Joan and I watched Perry Mason in the privacy of her room.

Trin asked, "Jane, where did you get the money?"

Joan quickly replied, "I never ask Jane where she gets her money. Only God knows!"

We had opened a mission in Chiapas, Mexico in collaboration with the Sisters from North Dakota and it came to our attention that they were in need of a jeep and dehydrated packages of food. I told Joan that I would obtain both if I could accompany the driver down to the mission. She was thrilled at the offer, and I soon began collecting money until I had the twenty-seven thousand dollars necessary to purchase the jeep. No one but God know where I got that money! Joan never asked.

I found it much different to deal with young Sisters than with the older Sisters. They had lived in a closed community since the day they entered as Postulents, and their problems tended to center around each other. When one of them came to me to discuss a problem it usually involved another Sister not sharing a text book, or not talking to her. Joan had arranged it so that I could stay overnight at Saint Agnes on Mondays to give me a break. Without fail, as soon as I was about to leave, one of the Sisters would need to talk to me. I took a course from a priest, who was a psychologist and warned us that, as Superiors, Sisters would expect to be able to talk to us for hours. "What you do is tell the Sister that you have an hour to give her. She will soon learn that she has to get right to the point."

The first week after the Sisters moved into the Juniorate, I was in the refectory and noticed that Sister Susan was talking to herself as she set the tables for dinner. The next day I asked the Sisters if they had ever seen Susan talk to herself. They assured me that they hadn't. I called the Novice Mistress and asked her the same question, but she confirmed that Susan never talked to herself and was quite normal. I finally went to Joan and told her that I thought Susan should see a psychiatrist. Joan made an appointment, and during her first session Susan told the psychiatrist that she did not want to be a nun. She went on to say that she would go to the Novice Mistress and ask to go home, but was told that it was the devil tempting her and she should stay!

When Joan heard of this she asked me to take all of the necessary steps for Susan to leave, if she so desired. When I met with her to inform her that she was free to leave the Congregation, Susan was visibly relieved. A smile crossed her face. The first step was to inform her parents that Susan and I wished to meet with them. Before traveling to Gilroy, where they lived, I made an appointment with the hair dresser and arranged for her to learn how to apply makeup. We then went shopping for clothes, accessories, and appropriate shoes. As we drove to Gilroy I could feel the joy that Susan was experiencing, knowing that she was going home to stay.

Susan's parents were delighted to see her, and told me that they never felt that Susan was happy in the convent. Parents have a way of recognizing their child's emotions. They were so grateful for all I did to have Susan ready to move back into secular life. "Sister, we believe that if you had been Susan's Novice Mistress you would have noticed that she was not happy and would have done something about it long ago," they told me.

I had arranged to have a party set up by the Sisters to celebrate Susan's decision and bid her farewell. We gave her luggage as a gift. It was unheard of that a Sister leaving the convent would have a party in her honor. You would only know that a Sister had left by her absence at breakfast the next morning. There was no opportunity to say goodbye to a Sister that you had lived with for years! It was amazing to see the change in Susan as we said our goodbyes. She was talkative and laughed heartily as the Sisters all shared funny stories about their times in the Novitiate.

I soon discovered that the Novice Mistress, who had insisted the devil was tempting Susan to leave, had an uncanny hold on the young Novices. They would ask to go back to the Novitiate to visit her each Saturday. After some time, they stopped asking and became attached to me instead. The breakthrough seemed to come when the Sisters individually came to me and said that they knew there was something wrong with Susan, but they were told to keep it to themselves. They said that the Novice Mistress had made implications that I lived a more relaxed rule. I was furious at this, but did not show it to the Sisters. I am sure the Novice Mistress had in mind the time that she confronted me over the fact that I had arranged a trip to Lake Arrowhead during Holy Week when I was still at St. Mary Magdalene.

"How could you go on vacation during Holy Week?" she asked.

"It was the most spiritual week I have ever spent!" I responded. Since we had no obligation in the parish during Holy Week, I thought it would be a perfect time for the Sisters to relax in the snow. We secured a lodge and saw to it that we attended all of the Holy Week services at the local church. Sister Augustine, who was in her eighties, experienced snow for the first time in her life. She told me later that it was the happiest week of her life.

During my first year at the Mother House, Sister Gregory went to Joan and told her that some of the Sisters thought I was conducting "Sensitivity Sessions" with them. Their concerns stemmed from the fact that I had attended a Sensitivity Course out of UCLA. The sessions were only open to CEOs, or business owners, but a visiting priest who had taken the course encouraged me to apply and arranged for an interview to see if I was eligible.

Sitting in full habit, the interviewer asked, "Sister, there may be people in the program who have had bad experience with nuns. Could you handle the criticism?"

I have been handling criticism all of my life!" I responded. I was approved.

On a Friday, the Sisters drove me to Lake Arrowhead, where the initial weekend sessions would be held. It was one of the worst snowstorms to hit the area in years, and a highway patrol officer had to drive in front of us so we could see the road. Unsure of what I was getting myself into, I had the Sisters stay at the lodge in Arrowhead and told them to drive by on Saturday when I would meet them at the fence if I wanted to leave!

At the registration table I was given a nametag and a packet containing a battery of tests that I was to complete by five-thirty. I was then shown to the cottage where I would be staying. I was greatly relieved that I would have privacy and would not be staying in a dorm.

When I returned to the lodge and sat down to take the test, a gentleman joined me and we quickly struck up a conversation. He shared with me his years in Catholic School. Thankfully, they were happy memories. I would soon learn that not all shared this sentiment! Having finished my test, I went into the room where they were serving drinks and snacks and saw that I was the only woman present.

After dinner we were assigned to groups of fifteen. We would remain in these groups for nine months. We would meet once a month at UCLA on Wednesdays. The content of the course that first evening came from participants who shared their life stories. One man informed me that he wasn't going to let me know that he was a Catholic because of his bad experiences with nuns in his youth. That night he called me and said, "Sister, if you need a ride to get to Mass tomorrow, I would be happy to take you." I had won him over!

By the time Sunday afternoon came, I felt as close to these men as I did to my own brother. It was the most significant course that I have ever taken. It opened the doors to a whole new way of relating to people. I learned to be comfortable, regardless of the conversation.

One day Joan came to me and said that she wanted the Sisters to go shopping for secular clothes to be worn on vacation. We were scheduled to travel to Boulder Creek in two weeks. I was surprised to meet with opposition on the part of Sisters. They expressed reservations about going out of the habit and shopping for secular clothes. I made them go anyway! That night we had a dress rehearsal. It was amazing to see their individuality surface in the outfits that they had selected. Nuns all look the same when dressed in full habit, with only their face and hands showing.

Our week at Boulder Creek was a wonderful experience of coming together as a community and getting to know each other better. The only mishap came when one of the Sister slammed the kitchen door shut, breaking the glass window. It was the day before we were to leave, and I didn't want to go until it was fixed. I could just hear the older Sisters saying, "The Junior Sisters wrecked havoc on the house at Boulder!" I called around and found a company that would replace the glass, but we would have to bring the door to the shop. It was quite a feat to remove the door and put it in the back seat. Thank God it fit! I then had the task of hanging the door and making sure it was secure.

During my time as Director of Junior Sisters, I came to the conclusion that the Sisters leaving the Novitiate should spend at least a year in a Mission House. I felt they needed the experience before making an informed decision regarding Final Profession. The Juniorate was really just an extension of the Novitiate. I shared this with Joan and she agreed with me. I was out of a job.

It was at this time that a decision had to be made regarding Saint Teresa's Parish School. When the freeway was put in, the convent and school were demolished and new land was found just two blocks from the church. A house on Missouri Street near the rectory was purchased and the Sisters were to make that the convent. Until the new school building could be built, the children and teachers were parceled out to other schools. It would be another year before the new school was ready for occupation. Joan approached me and shared her idea of building a school without walls. She had the faculty picked out, with Sister Daniel as principal and Superior. I was to be the vice-principal and eighth grade teacher.

I was sent to Portland Oregon, where I visited a school that had no classrooms but rather areas designated to each grade. The idea was that a child could move from grade to grade if she needed to refresh her memory in a subject she was having difficulty.

It was also during this time that Pope Paul VI asked religious women to go back to their baptismal names. How I rejoiced that I could sign my name as Jane, not Mary Catherine Laboure'! Sister Daniel was now known as Kathleen. It was a challenge to learn the names of the Sisters all over again.

We ended up teaching in the basement and choir loft of the church, until the new school was completed. I was assigned to the space above the church proper, which was an enclosed, stained glass window choir loft that overlooked the church below. When there was a funeral, we had to be as quiet as church mice!

When the smell of incense filled our "classroom" it was a sign that the service was coming to an end. I would carefully open the stained glass window and peek below to see if I could resume teaching without the fear of disturbing the service below.

The day finally arrived when we were to move into the new school on Arkansas Street. It was a two story building, with the fourth, fifth, sixth, seventh and eighth grades located on the bottom floor. Low bookcases separated the classes. The upper floor held the first, second and third grades. The proximity of the grades to each other facilitated the students moving to another grade for a remedial class. It took a great deal of coordination among the teachers, but we became a showplace for teachers who were interested in seeing how a school without walls operated. I would often look up and see adults peering over the bookcases, observing me teaching. It reminded me of a flock of birds landing on a fence.

My mission at St. Teresa's was coming to an end. In 1973 I agreed to move north to Ukiah.

PART III

11

My Years in Ukiah and Ministry to Native Americans

In February of 1973, I was attending the Silver Jubilee of Sister Mary Doreen Healy when I met Sister Patricia Marie, our Major Superior. I asked her how Sister Joan Murphy was doing since she wasn't at the celebration. A strange look came over her face and I said, "Is there something wrong with Joan?" She replied, "I need to talk to you, Jane". We went up on the stage of the auditorium behind the curtains. She proceeded to tell me that Joan had come to her and asked if she would transfer me to Pacifica where Joan was the parish Sister. She went on to say that Joan wanted to move out of the rectory and she and I could find a place and form a community. Joan no longer wanted to live alone. Patricia Marie told Joan that I was happy at St. Teresa's and that she couldn't move me. I said, "Sister Patricia Marie, for all that Joan has done for our community, anything she requests should be granted. I will go to Pacifica." Patricia Marie set a date the following Monday when Joan, she and I could meet in her office.

When I came home from the Jubilee, I told Sister Lucia that I was going over to Mass. "Jane, you went to Mass at the Jubilee." she said.

"I know but I want to go to Mass," I replied. Later she told me that I was white as a sheet! At Mass, I asked God to give me the grace to leave Saint Teresa's. That night at dinner I shared with the community that I had agreed to go to St. Peter's in Pacifica and live with Joan. The meal ended in tears. They would miss me as I would miss them.

On Monday morning I met with Patricia Marie and Joan. Joan gave me a hug and thanked me for saying, "yes."

It was decided that Joan would set up an appointment with Father Davenport, the pastor. Two days later Father came to the rectory and interviewed me. A date was set for me to be interviewed by the Parish Council. I can still picture the scene. The members of the council and myself met in a recessed area around the fireplace at the rectory. One lady asked if I would, like Joan had notoriously done, go out in a rowboat to stop the ship, Enterprise. My response was, "What I do with my time off is my business. I will do whatever I wish and that is not the parish council nor the pastor's business." Thanks be to God that I had the presence of mind to tell them that I was coming to form community with Joan and when would leave, I would leave. It was decided that I would come at the end of the school year.

Three weeks later I signed the contract to be the Director of Religious Education for St. Peter's Parish. The ink was hardly dry when I got a phone call from Joan saying that she resigned and would be leaving St. Peter's. The pastor had once again made a decision without input from the staff. She said that she would go wherever I went. I canceled the contract. For the first time in 43 years of religious life, I hadn't a clue where I would go. Every night I would go to my bedroom window, which overlooked the city of San Francisco. My tears were mingled with the glistening lights of the city. My nightly prayer was, "Dear God, tell me what I should do? Where should I go?"

Sister Patricia Marie came to see me and told me that I could go wherever I wished even out of state! At the first part of May, I got a call from Peter, the pastor, asking me to come to the rectory. There was someone there that he wished me to meet. As soon as I hung up, I headed for the rectory. On my arrival, I was introduced to Sister Margaret, a friend of Peter's. She was the Director of Religious Education for Santa Rosa and would be leaving. She advised me not to apply for that position but rather apply at either St. Bernard's in Eureka or St. Mary of the Angels in Ukiah. Those were her choices because they had good pastors. "Where in the world are Eureka and Ukiah?" I asked. She told me that both were north of San Francisco. Eureka would entail a five or six hour drive, but Ukiah was just two hours from San Francisco. Later I found out that my Sister, who lived in Rohnert Park, was just an hour drive from Ukiah. I could spend my day off with her. There was also a convent housing Mission San Jose Dominicans. I grew up with them and knew many of them. I would be able to live in the convent. This was a big drawing card since I knew I would not like to live outside a convent. It was finally decided that Margaret would contact the pastor in Ukiah and set up an appointment. The date was set for Holy Thursday, since school would be out for the Easter break.

I arrived in Ukiah around noon and drove to the convent where I would meet Sister Mary Louise, who was leaving the parish. We drove over to the rectory where the administrator, Father Roger, took us to lunch. I smiled when the secretary gave him the money for lunch. It wouldn't come out of his pocket. I soon learned that when it came to finances, the secretary wielded the power. Over lunch they proceeded to tell me what a wonderful parish Saint Mary of the Angels was with its devoted parishioners. I remarked that I felt I was being given a pitch similar to a car dealer trying to sell a car. No parish could be this wonderful. However, Mary Louise assured me that it was everything they were describing it to be. Later, I would see this to be true.

I told Father Roger that I would meet with the Sisters to see if they would agree to my moving into the convent. Roger assured me that they would be delighted. However I had to find this out for myself. After all I would be living with them. We went back to the convent and I met with the Superior, Sister Damian, who, after hearing I knew many of the Mission San Jose Dominicans, said that she would pray that I would come. On my ride back to San Francisco, I contemplated if I would go to Ukiah. It seemed to be God's will. The next day was Good Friday and I put a call into Roger to let him know that I would come to Ukiah. The secretary told me that he was in church for three hours. She went on to say that Roger sent me an eight page letter outlining why I should come to Ukiah. He returned my call and we set a date when I would come and sign the contract.

On May 31st, I drove to Ukiah and met up with Father Roger. The restaurant he had in mind was not open so we ended up at Fyord's on State Street. Before we even entered the restaurant, I signed the contract. After lunch I went to the convent and met all four Sisters. The principal, Sister Allyn, I had met briefly a few years ago while visiting Father Coleman. I immediately took a liking to her and was happy that I could look forward to living with her. Apart from Allyn, I knew no one in Ukiah except for Charlene, who had taught at St. Teresa's and now was teaching the sixth grade at St. Mary of the Angels. Shortly after meeting the Sisters, Mary Louise took me on a tour of the parish. We drove to Hopland, Redwood Valley and Potter Valley. Along the way she introduced me to a number of people. By the time we got back to the convent my head was spinning. How Was I going to minister to all of these areas? Ukiah alone was the size of San Francisco. It was 54 square miles. Not only did we tour the parish but she went over her programs with me. It was a very long day and I was happy to head home.

The day finally arrived when I would bid farewell to St. Teresa's.. I can still picture the Sisters framed in the doorway waving me off. I cried all the way, and when I stopped in Hopland for a cup of coffee the gentleman who served me wanted to know if I was alright. I shared with him that I was moving from a place I loved. He said, "Lady, I understand." He didn't charge me for the coffee. When I arrived at the school, the teachers were all gathered in the lunchroom. When

Vera Vargas, the secretary, handed me a McDonald's hamburger, she said, "Sister, you will love St. Mary's." She was so right. Vera was such a support to me all the years she was the secretary.

When Mary Louise was showing me around, she said, "Jane, I have neglected the Native Americans. I hope that you will reach out to them." It was then that I made up my mind to visit every Rancheria, introduce myself and encourage them to send their children to the Religion classes on Saturday. I spent the entire month of August visiting the Rancherias. It was obvious that they were given the worst land. It was arid and dry. The only break was a vineyard that was planted by some of the Indians. Their housing was deplorable. At times it was difficult to find a door. After my visits I concluded that there were few children of school age. The new generation, when they came of age, moved off of the Rancherias and got jobs in town or in Santa Rosa.

My visits paid off when I got a call from Nancy Williams of the Pinoleville Rancheria asking if I would moderate their elections for a Tribal Council. I knew then that I was trusted. Not only did I moderate their elections but they asked me to be an advisor to the tribal council. I readily accepted. With a new council in place, they wanted to retrieve the checkbook and statements from the lawyer that held them. I remember it was Good Friday when the new council and I walked up the stairs to the lawyer's office. After we were all seated, the inquires of the lawyer were addressed to me. I told him, "Don't look at me, but rather to the members of the tribe." When he only handed over the checkbook, we asked for the statements. He didn't think he still had them. We said that we would wait until his secretary located them. It was obvious that he was furious with us. However, the secretary finally came in with the statements. We went back to my office to look them over. Laughter soon followed. The previous Council had taken trips to Vegas and treated themselves to meals at expensive restaurants. I continued to advise the Council and soon became secretary of the Senior Nutritional Center where seniors received a hot meal. I was also able, after filling out a volume of forms, to get them a non-profit status.

One of the privileges I had working with the Native Americans was become a friend of Elsie Allen. Some of her baskets are on display at the Smithsonian in Washington D.C. I treasure the small basket that she weaved for me. It included a note expressing our friendship and gratitude for all that I was doing for her people. She gave me a rare interview in her home and allowed me to tape it. I was also allowed to take pictures of her family, which were framed and hung in the living room. She proceeded to tell me her story.

She would take a card table with a full tablecloth and put it by the river to pick the reeds she needed to weave the baskets. You were not to pick the reeds except for basket weaving. She said, "God put them there for us to weave our baskets." Her son was serving in the army during World War II and a government agent paid her a visit and offered her $5,000.00 for her property. She watched as he made out the check and handed to her. She said, "Sister, I took the check and tore it up in front of him and threw it back at him. I then told him to leave my house and to never return!" So many of the Indians were duped into selling their property at a mere pitance for what it was worth. On another occasion she told me that her little niece had watched the children playing at St Mary's School and wanted so badly to got to St. Mary's. Elsie called the school and spoke to the Sister Principal who told her that they had room in the third grade and to please come down and enroll her niece. She got to the school and was ushered into the principal's office.

"When the principal saw that I was Indian, she said that she was mistaken and that the class was full." Elsie went on to say, "Sister, I knew that it was because we were Indian. I understood that the principal feared that parents would take their children out of the school if they found out that an Indian child was enrolled. The Sisters couldn't afford to lose a child. They needed the money."

Tears came to my eyes at the wisdom and understanding that Elsie displayed. There was no anger or bitterness. She was a giant of a woman! I have to admit that I had anger that a Catholic School that teaches about Jesus would bar a little girl entrance because she was an Indian! I could only hope that I could be as forgiving and understanding as Elsie was when dealt an injustice.

Another beautiful Indian woman that I came to know was Ethel Burke. She was over 90 years old and raising her great grandchildren, most of whom were in diapers. I had visited her a number of times in her humble home on the Hopland Rancheria. I once asked her, "Ethel, how do you do it with all these children? There were six of them.

Her response was, "Sister, we do what we have to do." Another lesson learned!

One day she called me and told me that they had turned her water off and she feared for the children's health. I said, "Ethel, I'll be right out." When I arrived the children were out playing and Ethel took me inside, making sure that the door was open so that she could keep an eye on the children. I asked, "Ethel, can you give me the name of the person who shut your water off and do you have their phone number?"

She said, "Yes" to both. I asked to use her phone and called the gentleman responsible for shutting off her water. He answered, and I informed him that he was to turn the water back on because Ethel was caring for little children and she could not do without water. He told me that he didn't know where the valve was located.

I told him, "If you turned it off then you very well know where the valve is located. I will give you until 5:00 p.m. to turn the water back on or I will call the Ukiah Daily Journal and the Press Democrat informing them that you turned the water off on a woman over 90 yrs. old with small children. Believe me, it will make the headlines."

He hung up on me, but the water was turned back on at 4:50 p.m. I then asked Ethel how much her water bill was. She told me it was $20.00. I gave her the $20.00 and said if she ever ran short of money and couldn't pay the bill to please let me know and I would give it to her.

One day Ethel came in with some photos in her hand. She was crying. "Sister, some people asked me for pictures so that they could make copies to display in Grace Hudson Museum. They did not give me back the originals." I took the photos and said that I would retrieve the originals. After many phone calls, I tracked them down. When I handed them to Ethel, she gave me a big hug and thanked me profusely.

Among the items on the agenda of the Mendocino County Supervisors at this time was the issue of whether or not to renew the HUD contract for housing on the Rancherias. I met with the three tribal heads, who were all women, and made it clear to them that we had to go into the meeting united. There were to be no complaints that one Rancheria received more help than another or that one house got a new roof and some others didn't. We went into the meeting and I made the presentation. I described that two children had come down with pneumonia because the house they were living in was not properly insulated and the roof had not been completed. I noted many other problems and when it came to a vote they agreed that HUD should continue to do the work until all of the houses had been brought up to code. Ernie Bank, who was the chairman, said that he would personally monitor the work so that it was done properly. We left the meeting elated.

Once I had fulfilled my goal of reaching out to the Native Americans, I focused on the School of Religion.

12

Director of Religious Education and Planning Commissioner

Once I had fulfilled my goal of reaching out to the Native Americans, I focused on the School of Religion. When I met the principal, Sister Allyn, I shared with her my vision that all sacramental programs would be parish programs. That way we wouldn't have a First Communion Sunday for St. Mary' children, and another Sunday for the children of the School of Religion. She whole heartily agreed. Sr. Allyn and I worked well together. I always believe that when we go to a place where we know no one Jesus comes to us in the guise of a friend. Allyn was that friend.

When I first arrived and asked to see the CCD (Confraternity of Christian Doctrine) checkbook, I realized that there was no money in the checking account. I had to borrow a roll of stamps from the secretary at the rectory to send a letter to the parents informing them of the dates for Saturday classes and the cost of the text book. However, I made it clear that if they did not have the money at this time for the text, they were to enroll their children anyway. My belief was that no child should be denied a Religious Education because of money.

Given the fact that there were no funds in the School of Religion account, I began to create projects that would raise money. At this point the only money that came from the parish was the annual appeal on the first Sunday in September when a second collection was taken up. The pastor sent out a letter of appeal the week before. Only $700.00 dollars were raised. Not even enough to pay for the texts! A number of parishioners wanted to know if I received all of the money collected. I responded, "Absolutely." They then suggested that I write the letter and sign it. The pastor was in agreement and the second year brought in $2,000.00. The third year $4,00.00 and from then on in it rose to $7,000.00. Not only did I have money in the checking account, but I was able to open a savings account. I began to buy audiovisual aides and built up a library that contained more aides than the diocese had to offer. Not only did the School of Religion benefit but also St Mary's school.

At the time, I was responsible for all of the educational programs, including the elementary CCD classes, the junior high and high school programs, as well as adult education. I look back now and wonder how I ever accomplished it all!

Gratefully, the diocese adopted a Youth Ministry Program, which prepared young people to apply to parishes as Youth Ministers. The program was designed by Father Gary Timmons and Don Kimball. Bother were gifted youth workers.

When the first Youth Ministers were ready to apply to parishes, I asked the pastor to hire a young man named Doug, who don Kimball had highly recommended to me. Having a Youth Minister on board would relieve me of the youth programs and allow me to focus on adult education. Fearful that the pastor might say no, I informed him that I would have to resign as parish Sister, since I could no longer handle all of the programs for which I was responsible. He gamble paid off when Doug was hired.

The youth took to Doug immediately. Because he had majored in Education, he was a wonderful teacher. We became very close over the next three years and it was difficult for me when he decided leave the parish and go back to teaching. We went through several Youth Ministers, but none quite measured up to Doug.

The day finally came when I had enough funds to hire a principal for the School of Religion and eventually a director, which freed me to spend my time with the poor and homeless. This became advantageous to me, as I was beginning to form plans to open a community dining room.

In 1977, I was approached by the mayor's husband, Bob, who asked if I would be willing to serve on the Planning Commission for Ukiah. I told him that I would give it some thought and get back to him. The next day I went to the pastor and said, "I'm not asking you for permission, but I wanted to let you know that I was approached about serving on the City Planning Commission."

He responded, "Sister, all I ask is that you talk to Louie Zinna and Charlie Barra who are responsible for raising large sums of money to keep our parish school open." I agreed and met with Louie and Charlie to tell them that I was being considered for a place on the Planning Commission. Louie responded, "Sister, go for it, and I will pick up whatever responsibilities at the parish it takes you away from."

"Louie, does that mean you would teach the kindergarten?" I asked.

"Whatever it takes, I'll do it," he said.

Before being elected to the board, I was interviewed by one of the commissioners. "Sister, if you were on the Planning Commission at the time they were going to build the 101 Freeway, where would you put it?" he asked.

"I certainly would not have located it through the prime agricultural corridor of the city. I would have constructed it east at the foot of the mountains," I responded. He agreed with me and recommended that I be elected to the board.

I soon found myself seated at the city chambers with a placard that read "Sister Jane Kelly." We met once a month on Wednesday evenings. Prior to each meeting we were given a packet which contained the building requests that were to be voted on. I was appalled to see some commissioners opening their packets for the first time during the meetings. I made it a point to visit each site days in advance of the meetings to make sure I was familiar with the cite and the impact that the project would have on the neighborhood or agricultural land. I remember at one meeting when a board member asked what the green on the map represented. It was a park. It was somewhat frightening to me that the future development of the city rested on seven individuals, some who didn't even take the time to know the area.

The most memorable night of my time on the board came when a developer came to the meeting and proceeded to pass out his proposal to each of the commissioners. He was seeking approval for a housing development adjacent to a vineyard. In lieu of a park, he was offering a payment of $150,000 to the city. I looked at the proposal, realizing that if an eighth grade student had written it, he would have received a failing grade. It was full of poor grammar and misspelled words. I declared that I would never vote on a proposal that had been handed to me on the spot. We had just enough members present that night to constitute a quorum, and it was obvious that the other board members were ready to vote. I asked the Planning Director, "If I walk out, will that break the quorum?"

"Yes Sister," he told me. "But I hope you don't"

"Sister, if you walk out, I will make certain that you never serve on another board!" the Chairman of the Board added. I got up and walked out. The next day, the Ukiah Daily Journal ran a huge headline that read "Sister Jane Takes a Walk!"

A short time later the developer called me and asked if he could fly me to Davis to shot me and two other commissioners what he planned to build in Ukiah. I told him that would put us in violation of the Brown Act, which states that two or more commissioners can not meet with someone who was seeking approval of their building project. He cursed me and slammed down the phone!

At the next planning meeting, the developer came up to where I was seated and proceeded to hammer on the desk in front of me, demanding to know why I was so opposed to his project. The chairman pounded his gavel and told the man to take a seat. Since all of the commissioners were present, we took a vote. The proposed development was not approved. Two commissioners who were not present at the last meeting agreed with me that the development would hurt the adjacent vineyard. I found out later that the developer had left town. No one in the construction business would challenge him because he had a monopoly on building materials. They were delighted to learn that he had moved.

I was returning from Santa Rosa one night when my car hit gravel and I lost control. I went over the side of the road and would have landed in the river below if the passenger side of the car had not caught on the trunk of a tree. A CHP officer later told me that when he passed by he thought that anyone in the car must be dead. The roof had completely caved in. Thankfully, a couple was in the car behind me and pulled over to see if they could help. They called 911. I managed to climb out of the car myself, and when the ambulance arrived I refused to get in. I asked them to drive me to the convent instead. I must have used my "eighth grade tone" with them because they did as I asked.

Undoubtedly I was in shock and didn't realize the extent of my injuries. Sister Francis Clare answered the door when I arrived back at the convent. She sat me down in the dining room and declared, "Jane, I'm taking you to the hospital. Your collar bone is protruding!" At the hospital, they discovered that my collar bone was indeed broken and my legs were covered in severe bruises. I stayed at the convent until I was able to return to my own apartment. After this near death experience, I vowed that I would work less and take time out to smell the roses. It was a short lived promise!

One Friday afternoon, I was in my office when a knock came on the door. Much to my surprise, I opened the door to Father Ted Oswald and Father Gary Lombardi. Ted told me that Gary wished to talk to me. I was delighted to see Gary. I had met him in Petaluma when we were asked to give the students at St. Patrick's Seminary a talk on parish ministry. Secretly, I wished that he was our pastor. The present pastor was kind, but he never set goals or initiated programs. I had heard of all the programs that Gary had established at St. Bernards' in Eureka, including the Rite of Christian Initiation for Adults (R.C.I.A). It was a program designed to prepare people to be baptized into the Catholic Church.

After Ted left, Gary sat down, put his feet up on my desk, and told me why he wanted to see me. He informed me that the bishop has asked me to come to Ukiah as pastor! I used all of my persuasive powers to tell him why he should come to Ukiah. "Gary, I assure you that you will never regret leaving Eureka for Ukiah. The people are willing and ready to become involved in the parish ministry. Please call the bishop and tell him yes!" He left my office and went to do just that!

The parishioners in Ukiah were delighted with Gary. He initiated countless programs and worked with the staff on setting goals for the parish. He would take the staff to Tahoe for three days every year where he arranged for us to stay at a friend's house. It was a great time of bonding for all of us. We would spend one and a half days on setting goals after evaluating the accomplishments of the previous year. We would then head into town to try our luck at the casino and enjoy dinner together.

Gary and loved to cook and to entertain. Every Friday night he and I would cook dinner and host different groups of parishioners. It went a long way toward building community.

While Gary was in Europe on vacation, rumors began to circulate that he was going to leave Saint Mary of the Angel's parish for Saint Vincent's in Petaluma. As soon as he returned from his trip, he called me on his car phone and asked to meet with me as soon as he got to the rectory. Hanging up the phone, I knew he was going to tell me that he was leaving. I was devastated. We had become so close over the last few years. When I sat down in his office a short time later, he confirmed what I already knew. Amidst my tears I had the presence of mind to tell him that he needed to ask the bishop to come and break the news to the parish council, the finance committee and other parishioners. "Gary, they are going to be devastated."

"Jane, I didn't think this would be such a big deal," he replied. "I'll stay if need be."

"No, Gary," I said. "You would not have your heart in it. You need a change after nine years and are looking forward to a new appointment before you retire."

The parish mourned Father Gary's departure, but welcomed Father Hans Rought who took his place. It was quite a change, but Hans was a good priest. He was always open to the suggestions of the staff. I turned all of my energies to writing and ministering to the poor and homeless at Plowshares.

13

Plowshares

Little did I dream that a day in August of 1983 would change my life forever!

I was working in my office at school when I felt the presence of someone at the door and looked up. A young man was framed in the doorway with a binder tucked under his arm. I recognized him immediately. It was Martin Bradley. "Martin come in," I said. After he was seated, he blurted out, "Sister Jane, would you be interested in opening a community dining room for the homeless and the poor?"

"Martin, I have dreamed of this for years1," I responded. He opened the binder and showed me a picture of the old Social Services building on Main Street, which was for rent. I said, "Martin, you find the building and I will find the money." We set a date to meet and after he left, I sat back and said to myself, "Jane, where do you think you are going to find the money?" It then came to me that the pastors in Ukiah met every month as a ministerial group. I would ask if I could address them at their next meeting, which was scheduled for the following week. They agreed, and I addressed them regarding my request for funds to support a community dining room. I explained to them that they would no longer have to hand out food vouchers to poor people who came to their door. After the meeting, the representative from St. Mary's church pledged $300 a month, the Holy Trinity church pledged $100 and the Lutheran church $100. The church of the Nazarene could not afford money because they were a small congregation, but they would lend us their tables and chairs. The pastor of the Methodist church said, "Sister Jane, you will need seed money so we will give you a check for $2400—the sum of our two year pledge. We had the money!

Martin secured the building and began renovations with a volunteer crew. A group of people that Martin had assembled met in the dark, cold room in the newly acquired building. The group consisted of Martin, Debra Meek, Susan Crane, Mary Rice, Ann Near, Ginney Lindstead, Mr. & Mrs. Anderson and myself. Martin secured a sheet of paper near the window and we began to list the responsibilities that each would assume. I would be responsible for raising money and arranging for volunteers to cook and serve the meal. Martin would ready the building. Debra, Mary and Susan would acquire the necessary steam table, pots, pans and utensils. Ann Near would be our wise supporter. The Anderson's were leaving for a trip so could not commit themselves at that time. At the meeting Ginney turned to me and asked if I would still be here to oversee the operation of the dining room. I assured her that I would be here until they carried me out in a body bag. With that, she wrote a check for $300. It was our first personal donation.

Once again I turned to the churches to solicit volunteer cooks and servers. People told me that individuals would only be willing to work on the day that their church was responsible for the meal. Friends of Plowshares, under Debra's supervision, took Monday, St. Mary's took Tuesday, the Anglican church took Wednesday, the Presbyterian church Thursday and the Methodist church Friday. It didn't take long before volunteers chose the day that was best for them regardless if that was the day their church was responsible for cooking and serving.

On November 14, 1983 we opened our doors and invited our guests into the dining room. The first day we had more cooks and servers than guests. That soon changed and the numbers grew each day. Thanks to Faye Woodworth of the Ukiah Daily Journal who wrote feature stories with pictures, our donation base began to increase. Martin would crank out our *Advocate* on an old mimeograph machine, which solicited donations but more importantly wrote of the root causes of hunger and other justice issues. We purposely signed our title as Plowshares Community Dining Room and Peace and Justice Center. I remember when I went to get approval for our sign. I was told that we were advertising. I said, "Do you want us to add War to our sign?" When I went to the city attorney, he said that I could sue if we were not granted permission to keep the wording of our sign. Needless to say we were granted permission!

I look back now and ask myself, "How did we ever do it?" Our facility boasted one small sink and no kitchen. Each meal was cooked at a different location and Martin would pick up the meal and deliver it to Plowshares. Gratefully, we had a steam table to keep the food hot. In the beginning the cooks not only cooked but cleaned up afterwards at our small sink. I dreamed of the day when we would have our own kitchen.

While ministering to the poor and the homeless, we soon discovered that they had needs not only for meals, but gas, diapers, prescription medicines, etc. Martin and I were attempting to meet these many needs until one day we sat down after the dining room emptied and burst into tears. The demands were too great.

It was then that we decided that our goal was to provide a hot nutritious meal, nothing else. With that decision, we were at peace.

Everything was going along smoothly until a bombshell dropped! Francine, the realtor told us that the owner had sold the building and we were to vacate it by June 1, 1984. We both felt it was essential that we not interrupt the service so we packed up and moved to the park. The city granted us permission to serve in the park for two weeks. We had a portable potty moved to the cite. Aside from picking up the meal and transporting it to the cite, Martin, with the aide of one of our guests and his son, set up the tables and the chairs. Each day Martin and I would comb the area looking for a building. This went on for weeks.

When our two weeks in the park were up, we moved to Saint Mary's parking lot. There was a small building with a bathroom and an area with a sink. We could hook up the coffee pot to an electric outlet. The one blessing we had was the weather. Thank God it was not winter. Our volunteer cooks and servers stayed with us. I'll never forget the hottest day in August. Martin and I were out canvassing the area when we came across a vacant building on Cherry Street. It was an old shirt factory. Martin secured the papers and we met with one of the owners to sign the agreement. Our hopes were up until the owner said he would have to have his partner sign the agreement. When we met the next day, he informed us that the partner had other plans for the building. We were certain that he did no want to rent the building to house a community dining room for the homeless and poor. To this day that building is still vacant. Most people want to shelter the homeless and feed the hungry but not in their neighborhood!

Once again we hit the pavement in search of a building. After over an hour in the hot sun, I stopped and said, "Martin, I can't go on walking any longer in this heat." He encouraged me to walk one more block down State Street. We came to the corner of Luce and State Street. As soon as we turned the corner, a Church building loomed up on the right side of the street. It was like a mirage in the middle of the desert. We converged on the building and peered in every window to see the interior. It had a large room with another room set in the back that looked like it had been a kitchen. "Martin, we have found our building!" I declared.

Martin took off to find out who owned the building. He called me later to inform me. I immediately called the owner and prayed that he would answer the phone. Joy of joy, he answered on the second ring! I told him that we would like to lease the building. He said that he was waiting for a call from a man in the Bay Area who was interested in renting the church. He was to get back to him by 2:00 p.m. the following day. At 2:01 p.m. I called and found out that the other interested party had not called. We could lease the building for $350 a month. "Should I bring you a check now," I asked?

"No, Sister. Tomorrow will be soon enough." We had a building!

Martin assembled a crew and started the renovation of the building while Debra, Susan and Mary purchased the pots, pans and utensils for the kitchen. We received a stove from the local fire department and the Indian Nutritional Center, who were both replacing their stoves. A local cabinet maker left a sheet of paper with 20 numbers listed down the side of the paper. I was to list what we would like him to do. The first request was to build a block table in the middle of the kitchen with shelves under it and cabinets and shelves in the kitchen area and the storage room.

Within a week we were ready to open the doors to our guests! What a luxury to have our own kitchen and no longer transport the meal to the dining room. It soon became apparent that we needed a walk-in refrigerator to store the produce and other perishables that Roy gathered daily from the local markets and bakery. I wrote a hundred letters to people I felt could lend me a $1000, telling them I would repay them on a first come basis. In two weeks we had enough to purchase the unit. Only one person requested to be paid back. I remember receiving a check for $7000 and was concerned that the person could not afford it since the address was in a local R.V. park. When I called to express my concern, the lady responded, "Sister, my husband and I have been in the restaurant business most of our lives and know you must have a walk in refrigerator." I was able to acquire a walk in freezer using the same approach. We were able to freeze donated meat and turkeys that we received at thanksgiving. With both additions we had a well equipped kitchen.

To enhance our dining room, one lady picked up flowers from our local flower shop and arranged them on each table. We prided ourselves on the fact that we were a community dining room. I would cringe when anybody used the word "soup kitchen." I would always tell our guests that we had the best restaurant in town. The price was right and you didn't need a reservation. Our daily meal was a five course, hot and nutritious meal. We had a policy that families, the elderly and the handicapped were served first.

I remember one day that I noticed a little family of four waiting on the bench to go into the dining room. When I returned from an errand, I noticed that the father and one of the children were sitting on the bench. I went up and asked, "Why aren't you eating with the rest of the family?"

The father answered, "Sister, we only have two pairs of shoes so we had my wife and daughter go in first." It tugged at my heart. I dashed off to Dorcas

House, which is a free clothing store, and came back with shoes and socks for all four. There were so many heart wrenching stories told at Plowshares. Another time, the Chef, George brought out a cutting board with a large roast on it. He asked each guest what cut of meat they wanted. He was even decked out in a chef's hat and white apron! A mother was in line with her daughter and I overheard her to explain to the little girl, "Honey, this is a roast."

Ever since we opened our doors on Main Street, I wanted to take the homeless children home and put them in a tub and wash them clean! We needed a place where homeless people could shower and wash their clothes. This was not only for hygiene reasons, but so adults could be presentable for a job interview. What tipped the scale for me as to the importance of this was when I found out that a homeless woman had secured a job in a convalescent hospital and would come in early to sneak a shower. When it was discovered, she was fired!

An opportunity for me to get word out to people that I wanted to add a Personal Care Center to Plowshares came one Thanksgiving Day. A journalist from the Ukiah Daily Journal came to St. Mary's where we were setting up for the Thanksgiving meal. Our dining room would not hold the expected numbers. He asked if he could ask the volunteers what they wished for this Thanksgiving. I agreed but only if I could go first. My wish was that we had a facility where homeless people could shower and wash their clothes. The wish appeared in the next day's edition of the paper. Three days later I received a call from our director telling me that money had been donated for the Personal Care Center. In my mind, I thought ten or twenty dollars. The donations came to $4.000! I considered this a mandate.

I went to every realtor in town to see if there was a building available, but there were none. I woke up one morning and said to myself, "Jane, build it at Plowshares." That way people could take their showers and wash their clothes while waiting to eat. At a reasonable hour, I called Fontaine McFadden, who was in the process of renovating a house. I shared with her my plan to build a Personal Care Center at Plowshares. She informed me that she was meeting with her contractor and electrician and would meet me at Plowshares in fifteen minutes.

When they arrived, I pointed out where I thought we could construct the addition. The electrician was most kind. He said, "Sister, it would be better on the east side of the building since that is where the electrical outlets are." The contractor informed me that the start up cost would be about $20,000. I called the owner and he gave permission for the addition to be built. He offered to loan me the $20,000, but I told him that I would raise the money..

Once again I asked myself, "Jane, where are you going to get the money?" I then remembered that my congregation had a fund that gave grants for projects that help the poor. I filled out the form and sent it to the committee. About a week later I received a check from Sister Mary Catherine King. I thought how generous of her to donate $20 to Plowshares. I called her to thank her and she asked me if I read the amount of the check. The check was for $20,000! I had forgotten that Catherine Mary was on the Committee that approved requests for grant monies. We were in the money!

Shortly after, I was at a meeting where a man named Robert Clark was in attendance. He passed his card up to me, asking to meet me after the meeting. After the meeting, Robert told me that every year the North Coast Building Association took on a project and that they had chosen our project this year. What a gift Robert proved to be. In October we broke ground and within the next three weekends we had a "barn raising" and the frame was put into place. Needless to say, I was there every day to observe the progress and to thank the volunteer crews. Bob Axt, the architect, did a superb job in making the most of our floor space. I told him that I wanted the center to be a warm and welcoming building with wood paneling and tiles in the showers. I did not want it to look like a gymnasium. The workers were invited to have lunch at Plowshares, and on weekends I would take orders for sandwiches and cold drinks.

The building was on its way but I had to decide who would oversee the operation. Once again, God came to the rescue. A Franciscan Nun named Sister Thelma was living in Ukiah to take care of her elderly parents and was looking to do something with her spare time. I asked to meet with her. Over lunch I told her about the Personal Care Center that would be opening the first of February and informed her that we needed a director to oversee the program. She immediately agreed to take on the job. I had shelves installed in the Center to hold towels, wash cloths, soap and shampoo. Thelma came in and stocked the shelves and made curtains for the windows. It became her domain. She ran a tight ship. No guest exited the shower without first wiping it down. Rules for using the washers and driers were faithfully adhered to.

We soon added an examining room where a doctor and nurse would come once a week to examine any guest that requested to see the doctor. A telephone was installed for our guests and they could give out that number when being interviewed for a job or if they needed to make an emergency call. As always, homeless people used our address to receive mail. A barber chair was donated and a woman came three times a week to do haircuts The goal was to help our guests to look presentable when going for a job interview. We have had many a success story where a homeless person secured a job and was able to get into housing.

One of the drawbacks to our facility was that we were only allowed to be open Monday through Friday, and then only from 11:00 a.m. to 12:30 p.m. We were allowed to open the Care center at 8:00 a.m. to 7:00 p.m. to accommodate those who were going to work and needed to shower. For this reason, we realized that we needed to seek another location and enlarge our facility. Sister Mary Ann Curran's sister willed a $275,000 donation to our building fund. Over the years we added to that sum and came up with enough money to buy property on South State Street. Our goal was to raise two million dollars! To date we have almost reached that goal. Bob Axt is the architect and we have sent out bids to contractors. We will break ground in the spring of 2006.

I look back to August of 1983 when Martin and I had no money, no building and no experience. Now we are engaged with a two million dollar facility! With God all things are possible. I believe if you can dream it you can make it a reality.

14

Catholic Nun Blows the Whistle

I'll never forget the dreaded feeling when I awoke one Sunday morning to read the headline "Catholic Nun Blows the Whistle" in huge letters across the front page of the Press Democrat on January 22, 1999.

The story told of how Sister Jane Kelly had tried for two years to have Father Jorge Hume Salas of the Santa Rosa Diocese removed from active ministry as a priest. Bishop Patrick Ziemann had asked me to be Jorge's supervisor. He was a young man from Costa Rica who had applied to become a priest in the Santa Rosa Diocese. Bishop Ziemann had accepted him and assigned him to Saint Mary of the Angel's parish in Ukiah where I was stationed.

When I received a call from the parish secretary that the newly appointed bishop wished to see me, I hurried over to the rectory, anxious to meet the new bishop. Bishop Ziemann met me at the door with a huge bear hug and told me that he had a favor to ask of me. "Sister, I would like you to be the supervisor of a young man, Jorge, who will be in residence to see if he qualifies for priesthood."

"Bishop," I quickly responded. "I do not speak Spanish and I don't know how much English Jorge speaks."

"Not to worry, Sister. Jorge will be taking English classes and he does know some English." I went on to say that I had no experience in supervising a seminarian. The bishop assured me that he was going to set up instructional classes for the people he was asking to supervise seminarians.

Beginning to weaken, I asked the Bishop for Jorge's psychological test results and his transcripts. The Bishop told me that they did not have psychological tests in Spanish. "Bishop, they had tests in Spanish before they had tests in English," I cried. He dismissed this comment with a wave of his hand and went on to say that they did not have a copy of Jorge's transcript. I found both of these facts odd.

"Bishop, without a psychological profile, Jorge could be a psychopathic liar of killer," I said. How prophetic these words would later prove to be! Reluctantly, I agreed to supervise Jorge. Little did I dream it would later change my life forever.

I met with Jorge weekly and we would spend sometimes three hours conversing. I was never sure if he fully understood me. These sessions became a drain on me because I had to confront Jorge so often. The second time we met, he showed me a bank book. He had opened an account into which he was going to deposit money from his Youth Program fees. I told him, "Jorge, all accounts have to go through the parish. Cancel the account and talk to the pastor when he returns from his vacation." Jorge left immediately for the bank.

At morning Mass, I noticed that Jorge got as close to the altar as he could. Again I confronted him and said, "Jorge, you should be down with the congregation."

His response was, "Sister, I want to be as close to Jesus as I can."

"Jorge, Jesus is just as close to the people in the pews." Later, I realized he was trying to learn how to "Mass!"

It became evident to the pastor and me that Salas was not flexible. He demanded certain requirements of the parents whose children were in the Spanish First Communion program. The parents were to attend the Sunday morning classes without exception. One mother explained to him that she worked on Sunday and was a single parent who could not afford to take time off work. He dismissed the child from class. When I heard of this, I was furious! Both the pastor and I pointed out to Jorge that he had to be flexible and that his lack of flexibility concerned us. He reversed his decision and admitted the child back into the program.

I was beginning to suspect that Jorge would do whatever it took to be approved for ordination. However, Jorge had unbounded energy and formed a youth group which included a soccer team that won a number of trophies. Over one hundred adults were commissioned as lectors, Eucharistic Ministers and Catechists. During Holy Week, he organized a live stations of the cross which ended up in the Church parking lot where three huge crosses were erected and three men were lifted up and hung on the crosses. On the Feast of Our Lady of Guadalupe he led a parade of hundreds of Hispanics who processed to the fair grounds for Mass. Both the pastor and I were impressed.

One day, while the pastor and I were meeting in the pastor's office, Jorge appeared and announced that the bishop was going to ordain him a deacon. It was the final step before priesthood. I was astounded that the bishop had not consulted with me regarding Jorge's eligibility much less consulted with the pastor!

Nine months later Jorge announced once again to the pastor and me that the bishop was going to ordain him a priest. It literally blew my mind. Jorge had never attended any classes on theology or Liturgy and never made a retreat!

One week before Jorge was to be ordained the bishop was having dinner at the rectory and called me into the sitting room after dinner. He asked, "Sister Jane, do you think Jorge is a psychopathic liar?"

"Bishop," I responded, "I have no idea."

Ziemann then said to me, "If you don't want me to ordain him, just say the word."

"Bishop, don't lay that on me," I responded. "If you have doubts then don't ordain him."

Jorge was ordained. All of his zeal quickly vanished. The Youth Group was abandoned. Catechists were dismissed and replaced by two young Hispanic men, one of whom spent nights with Jorge. There were no Holy Week Living Stations of the Cross and the ministry sessions ceased. Suddenly Jorge, who hardly had two nickels to rub together, was sporting a new car, designer clothes, and a computer, not to mention other electronic devices.

I went to the pastor, Hans, and asked, "Where is Jorge getting all of this money?"

The pastor said, "Priests receive a salary and do not have many expenses."

"Hans, no priest ordained in less than a year makes this kind of money."

It didn't take long before I discovered that he was stealing money from the collection and selling religious articles. It soon became obvious that Salas was also molesting young Hispanic men. This was brought to the attention of the Bishop. (The whole story of Jorge's deception and criminal acts are described in my book Taught to Believe the Unbelievable A New Vision of Hope for the Church and Society.)

The Bishop came immediately to met with the Parish Council, Finance Committee and the Parish Staff along with the Chief of Police. He swore them to secrecy and whisked Jorge away. I knew what he would do, so I did not attend the meeting. The power of the Bishop was evidenced in the fact that not one person spoke of the matter.

For two years, I went through every Church channel to have Jorge removed, but to no avail. I finally went public with the story.

15

Going Public

My decision to go public with the story was one of the most frightening and painful decisions of my life. It was only after I read the numerous letters to the editor that appeared in the *Press Democrat* in reaction to the cover story, as well as the piles of personal letters and cards that I received, that it came home to me that so many people understood what it meant for me to openly criticize a member of the Church hierarchy.

One of those people was Don Hoard, the father of a boy who had been sexually abused years before by a priest in Humbolt County, California. In a letter to the editor in the *Press Democrat* on January 30, eight days after my story made the front page headlines, Mr. Hoard wrote, "For this lady to do what she's done is mind-boggling. If you don't have a Catholic background, I don't think you can conceive of the amount of courage it took." It was this kind of support and appreciation that sustained me through those trying days.

The sheer volume of newspaper articles and letters that appeared in response to my story made it obviously that my actions had touched many, many people. As I sorted through it all, it slowly began to dawn on me that my public statement had resonated deeply and broadly in people across the nation—people who knew, either instinctively or through direct, painful experience, that the power and the authority of the Catholic Church had taken on a life of its own, and that it did not always serve the best interest of the Church's followers.

I was literally inundated with requests for interviews from newspapers, magazines and T.V. channels. My life had taken on a new way of being.

My life further changed when I made the decision to write a book, not only describing the story of Jorge and the cover up by Bishop Ziemann, but my realization that I had been taught to believe the unbelievable. This whole experience forced me to re-examine everything I was taught, both as a child and an adult. It freed me up, and I wanted to free others up as I had been.

Because my book was controversial, I could not secure a publisher, so I decided to self-publish. Within 10 days of its publication, I was offered a contract. Over 1,000 books had been sold and I was busy with book signing commitments. No less than 300 people attended the book signing sessions!

I have also sold the movie rights to the book. Another film company contacted me to do a documentary on my life. It became quite clear to me that my book had made an impression on those who read it.

One Sunday after Mass, I heard a voice calling my name. I turned but did not recognize the woman hurrying toward me. When she caught up with me she said, "Sister Jane, my sister pointed you out as the Sister who wrote the book. My sister gave me a copy and told me that I must read it. It changed my life. My son is homosexual and I had dismissed him from my life. After reading your chapter on homosexuality, I called my son and we are back communicating!"

One day I received a call from Philip Kavanagh, M.D. who had written an endorsement for my book, which appeared on the cover. He asked if I would have breakfast with him since he would be passing through Ukiah. I was delighted since I wanted very much to meet him. We entered the restaurant at 9:00 a.m. and didn't leave until 12:00 p.m. As soon as we were seated and placed our order, Philip looked at me and said, "Jane, why did you write the book?"

"Philip, I did not write it for money. I wanted to free people the way that I had been freed," I responded.

He then looked me in the eye and said, "You have been ordained from all eternity to write this book but you must know that your life will never be the same!" How true his words proved to be.

The words that Dr. Kavnagh wrote that appeared at the front of the book were as follows:

> Sister Jane Kelly is a healer. In this book, she exercises the Courage to identify and make public the addictive behaviors and lies that keep the Church in the Dark Ages. This book's vision, while controversial, gives us all a chance to look more closely at our own lives, seeking deeper self-awareness and greater awareness of our spiritual identity. Perhaps in the process we will all demand more of our religious leaders.

PART IV

16

My Waterloo

One Friday afternoon a friend brought over a Mexican dinner complete with Margaritas. Later that evening I was in the living room watching the news when I noticed that the fire was low. I got up and went out to the front porch to get a log. I lifted a log and didn't realize that it was holding up the stack. When I picked it up, the whole stack crashed down on my left arm. I quickly ran into the bathroom, grabbed a brown towel to wrap the wound and drove to the Emergency Room. They took my blood pressure, which was normal, and then told me to wait for the availability of a doctor. As soon as one was available I was ushered into a cubicle. They took a sample of my blood, which puzzled me since that never happened before when I came to the Emergency with a wound. The doctor came and dressed the wound. It was deep and he informed me that I might need plastic surgery. Gratefully, that didn't prove to be the case.

When he was finished, the doctor told me that he did not want me to drive home. I said, "Doctor, I drove myself here and I am capable of driving home."

Much to amazement he said, "Sister your blood alcohol level is three times the normal!" I couldn't believe it.

"Doctor, I haven't been drinking!" I said. Then it dawned on me. I drank Margaritas! He must have smelled alcohol on my breath. Then I heard a familiar voice in the cubicle next to me. It was a parishioner named Harold (not his real name). When I asked him to drive me home he readily agreed to take me, but first wanted to say hello to my doctor who was a friend of his. Harold came back and said, "I don't know why the doctor wants me to drive you home, Jane."

We arrived home and I asked Harold if he could pick me up the next day and drive me to the hospital to pick up my car and have my dressing changed. I was grateful that he agreed.

Two weeks later I went down to St. Teresa's for a Covenant meeting. The next morning at breakfast Sister Lucia said that Harold had called the Mother House informing them of my blood alcohol level and that the President and the

Vice President were coming that morning to speak to me and to inform me that I was to go back to the Mother House. "Lucia, I will leave the Order before I will go to the Mother House!" I told her.

Shortly after the President and her companion arrived, we met in the kitchen and they told me that they wanted to have a doctor go over my medications. He was stationed at a hospital in Burlingame. I agreed and we took off for the hospital. I questioned why they put my overnight bag in the car. I simply dismissed it as a precaution should Kath and Lucia not be home when we got back. As we proceeded to the hospital, I repeatedly asked if we were going to a normal hospital and if I was going to be seen by a doctor in the hospital to review my medication. They assured me each time that I was going to a normal hospital.

When we drove up to the entrance I saw in bold lettering *Emergency Psychiatric Wing*! I froze. They assured me that we had to register in the emergency room to make an appointment with the doctor. "You had two weeks to make an appointment," I said.

"Yes, but I didn't," replied my Superior.

When we got in, I went to the desk and asked if a doctor could change my dressing. "First things first," the receptionist said. She put a hospital wrist band on me and told me to be seated.

Soon after, an Amazon of a woman appeared at the door adjacent to the receptionist's window and bellowed out, "Sister Jane Kelly, come here." My two companions got up and were told that they were to stay. She punched out some numbers to open the door. I realized it was a combination and when we got to the second door she used a key to open it. It suddenly dawned on me that we were entering a lock-up facility. When she opened the door I registered shock! People were walking around in their robes and slippers, obviously out of it. She ushered me into a small room and said that she would return shortly.

"They are having me committed!" I told myself.

When the woman returned I told her, "You can not keep me here."

Her response was, "Sister, we have no intention of keeping you against your will." She went on to say that she needed to get a release form to be filled out before I left. I felt like I was being released from jail. My companions had lied to me and tried to trick me into being committed. I vowed that I would never believe them or trust them again. After my release, the President said she would compromise. I was to either agree to be committed, or my car would be taken away. What was being compromised? It was a clear either-or proposition. I began to realize that this woman lived in a black and white world with no gray area. All issues were reduced to either-or.

Before we left the hospital, I was able to go to the main hospital building to have my dressing changed. After lunch we drove to the Mother House where Sister Kathleen and Lucia would meet me to take me to St. Teresa's. Tearfully I emptied my car and handed over the keys. This was a Monday and I was told that I could not return to Ukiah until Friday. Why the wait? I realized it was a way for my Superior to say that she had the power and I had to obey.

Kath and Lucia drove me home and thoughtfully took me to Safeway to pick up any groceries I might need. I was in a rural area that did not have public transporation. I had to go to the doctor Monday through Friday to have the dressing changed. If I called the night before, I could arrange to have Dial-a-Ride pick me up, but then I would be forced to wait an hour or two to be picked up to go home. I was too tired to arrange a pick-up to take me to water therapy and then wait for a ride home.

One day I was waiting for Dial-A-Ride to take me to the doctor and it didn't arrive, so I began to walk, praying that someone I knew would drive. No one did. I kept walking and stopped in a Real Estate office on Gobbi St. to see if someone could give me a ride. They said, "Sister, I can't leave the office." I continued to walk and eventually reached Luce Avenue where Plowshares was located. I prayed "God, please let someone be in the parking lot." I literally stumbled and fell against a van that was parked. By this time I was sobbing.

Thankfully the staff and Michael, a volunteer, were standing out in the parking lot. Michael came right over and helped me into his van. When I told him that I was on my way to the doctor, he said, "Sister I will take you." The other staff members said that all I had to do was call and they would provide a ride. Michael took me to the doctor, waited and drove me home. He made sure that I was safely in the house.

My next stressful episode came when it was raining and I wanted to get starter logs for my fireplace. I waited for the rain to abate and then set off with my shopping cart. The store was a little less than a mile so I thought that I could get there and back before the next downpour. Not so! I had just exited the store when the heavens opened up. As I went to step off the curb, I heard a voice call out, "Sister Jane, stay there!" It was Julie, a volunteer from Plowshares. She drove up next to me and said, "Get in." She placed my cart in the trunk and drove me home. She brought the logs in and set one in the fire place with the words, "Get out of your wet clothes."

By this time I had had it! No one in authority can order you to do something that threatens not only your physical health, but also your psychological health. I called Ken Fowler, a car dealer in town that I had known for years and said, "Ken, I need a car today."

He said, "Sister, give me thirty minutes and I will get back to you." True to his word he got back to me and said, "Sister, I have a car for you. I will send a driver over to you to bring you to the dealership. You probably know him, Efran." I said I had known him since he was in diapers! Efran picked me up and Ken showed me the car. It was a 2003 Corvelle with 40,000 miles on it. It looked brand new. The price was $8,000. I had $2,000 to put down and could afford to pay $257.00 for a car loan.

When all of the paperwork was complete, I told Efram that I needed car insurance to drive the car off the lot. He asked me what my car insurance was from my last vehicle. I told him that he would have to call the Mother House. He reached the President and she informed him that I did not have permission to drive. "Efram, get on the phone and arrange for car insurance." I told him. In a matter of minutes, I was signing papers for car insurance. At 6:00 p.m., in a torrent of rain, I pulled out of the lot and was headed home with my own car.

I called the President to inform her that I had ought a car and was making the payments. I told her that I did it for survival.

Orders came from the Mother House informing me that I was to go to a psychological institute to be evaluated. I backed out of two programs because they were out of state, and I was fearful that they would keep me for a matter of months. One brochure stated that the minimum stay was nine months. However, I was told that would not be so. There was a program that entailed just six days for the evaluation. I agreed to go

17

I Flew Over the Cuckoo's Nest

I was wary of going for an evaluation at a place I knew nothing about, and fearful that they would keep me for an indefinite time. But I was assured by the President that it was only a six day period of evaluation. My good friend, Sister Mary Jane Floyd, encouraged me to go and get it over with. The date was set in February, and I was picked up by two of the sisters and taken to the Mother House on a Wednesday. I was to fly out on a Saturday morning, but they wanted me there ahead of time lest I back out after they bought the ticket! The few days I spent at the Mother House before my departure was a wonderful time to be with the Sisters.

I rose at 3:00 a.m. to be picked up by the President and a companion who would travel with me to Toronto, Canada. We arrived at the airport in time to fly out at 6:00 a.m. My companion thoughtfully packed us a lunch and secured isle seats. We arrived at the facility in Toronto at 4:00 p.m. It was 7:00 p.m. Pacific time. We had flown through three time zones. Thankfully it was arranged that there would be a wheel chair waiting for me at each stop. I had ruptured discs in the lower back. I didn't bother to take pain medicine, since I was not in pain. Each day I would go to water therapy and it worked wonders.

When we arrived at the center, I was interviewed and given a test to see if I was suicidal. I was also asked if I had any sharp instruments with me. I was tempted to say that I had left my guns at the front desk and that I would relinquish my knife to the front desk as well. However, I restrained myself since sarcasm would not benefit me at this time. I had made up my mind that I would follow the rules and do what I was told so that it wouldn't be recommended that I return for a 6 month stay.

The ratio of men to women at the facility was 3 to 1. At dinner I remarked that the ladies would have it made if we had a dance. My companions said that there was line dancing once a week. However, I soon learned that when you were there to be assessed you did not have the privileges granted to the residents. You could not go dancing, use the swimming pool, the computer, the library or leave the grounds. We were told beforehand that we were not to bring a cell phone or a lap top. They did give us a $5.00 phone card. I used mine to call Sister Mary Jane each evening. She graciously put up with my tears! All I wanted to do was to go home and get back to my water therapy.

On Monday morning, those who were to be assessed met with the resident psychiatrist who explained the program and gave each of us a packet which held psychological tests and blank binder paper to write our autobiography. We were to complete the tests and autobiography by dinner time. I started at 9:00 a.m. and took only a bathroom break and a break for lunch. I completed the written tests by 4:00 p.m. but did not have the energy to write the autobiography. I took the materials and handed them to the woman at the desk.

We were to be interviewed by a nurse, an addiction councilor, a Spiritual Director and a psychologist. My psychologist, Henry (not his real name), was the person who determined if you should return for six months of treatment. I could begin to feel pain in my back as I stood up from filling out the questionnaires.

The rules stated that we were not to give our last names, touch each other, enter another person's room or ask anyone why they were here. The first night at dinner, I broke the first rule and introduced myself as Jane Kelly. I was seated with five priests who in turn told me their last names. We seemed to end up at the same table for meals and became friends. Often, at the end of the day, we would meet in the corridor and share a hug. However, we never went into each other's room. By the third day they were sharing with me why they were there and asking for prayers.

We were at dinner one night and my friends shared with me that on the previous Saturday, I was just a name on the board. Since being at the facility, I had turned the place upside down!

Tuesday morning I woke up and could hardly get out of bed. The pain in my back was excruciating and it took all of my strength to get dressed. With the help of the cane, I was able to get to the nurse's office The doctor was standing in the doorway talking to the nurse. They took one look at me and exclaimed, "Sister, you are in terrible pain! Come in and we will give you something for the pain."

I was so relieved since I didn't know how I would be able to go through all of the interviews that day. The nurse told me to come back twenty minutes before I was to be interviewed by the psychologist. It would be a grueling experience. She was not exaggerating. At 11:00 a.m. I began the five hour sessions with Henry. With great effort, I managed to seat myself. The battery of tests included the ink blot test, the word association test, the completion of sentences and finally the block test. I was given a picture and then I was to duplicate it with the blocks. I pushed the blocks back to Henry and said that I couldn't do it. I needed to retire to my room and get lie on the bed. Again struggling, I managed to stand up and leave the room.

The next day Henry informed me that I had failed the test. I said, "You mean the one with the blocks?"

"Yes. You have difficulty with motor skills," he told me. I asked if he could give me an example. He said when you I was at the Chicago airport I had difficulty getting out of the bathroom stall. I burst out laughing, but was quick to say that I wasn't laughing at him.

"I have a title for my next book," I said. "Be Sure that You Can Get Out of a Bathroom Stall."

He responded, "Is that a joke?"

"Yes, Henry that is a joke." This man had no sense of humor. He was forever moving in his chair and had an eye twitch, which made me twitch too. Apart from my impaired motor skills, he informed me that I had poor memory. I told him that this was not in my realm of experience.

"You are a proud and an accomplished woman. You wrote a book and find it hard to admit that you can't remember," he told me. The interview turned into an interrogation. All that was lacking was a bare light bulb overhead. He kept repeating that I could not remember.

I finally said, "Henry, if you want me to say that I can't remember, I'll be happy to do so. Again, I just want to end the session and get off my back." With that, I struggled up and left.

That night I decided that I wanted to evaluate Henry and the program. I left him a note requesting fifteen minutes of his time to share my evaluation. The next day I shared with my friends that I had left a note on Henry's door requesting time to evaluate him and the program. They said, "Jane, you are out of your mind. He is the one that will determine if you need to return!" They went on to say that they wished that they had the courage to do the same.

My response was, "I can assure you that I will not return regardless of Henry's recommendation." I went on to say that I could not leave without sharing my views of the program in hopes that they would take them under consideration.

I met Henry at lunch and asked if he would have time to see me. He told me that he was very busy, but would try to work me in. I had to smile at this because he had told me previously that if I needed to see him, he would be available. Just before dinner at 4:45 p.m. I was paged. Henry could see me. Undoubtedly, he wanted to keep it to fifteen minutes.

On my way back from lunch, I saw Michael sitting in the foyer. I said, "Michael, I thought you were to begin the Assessment program this morning." He told me that the chancery office had not sent his records so he couldn't begin the process until they did. I told Michael, "Call the chancery office and tell them if the records aren't faxed within the hour, you will go home."

Later that day I met him and he said, "Sister, it worked! They faxed the records." This was a strategy that I learned from a Sister in my Congregation, Sister Annetta. She said if you want an answer to a request, inform the recipient that if you don't hear from them, it means "yes" to your request. It never fails.

Promptly at 4:45 p.m. I was knocking on Henry's door. As soon as I was seated, I expressed my gratitude to him for seeing me. I then began to reflect back on my experiences since I came to the institute.

"Henry when I came into your office, it was obvious that I was in a great deal of pain. You made no move to get up and help me into the chair. You started off by questioning me for an hour. I felt that it was an interrogation rather than an interview. You proceeded with multiple tests that lasted for five hours. You never once made reference to my pain. Any psychologist knows that you don't test a person who is on pain medication. It impairs a person's reflexes. The staff are under constraints, since they have only one hour to ask the 100 questions of the client. There is no time for dialogue. Furthermore, to expect a client to answer all of the questions posed by the battery of tests in one day is overwhelming. As to the institute, the location is beautiful, the food excellent and the staff and residents are gracious and most helpful. When it was seen that I was in pain leaning on a cane for support, a resident would carry my tray through the line, help me to get seated and then take my tray away. Whenever a resident saw me struggling to go up or down the stairs, they were there to help me."

Having completed my evaluation I left and went to dinner. The next day, Thursday, was a day free of interviews. I approached the resident psychiatrist and asked if I could go into town and get my hair done. He told me that I wasn't permitted to leave the grounds. He was sorry and hoped that I understood. He was so sweet. "Sister, your hair looks just fine," he added.

The next day would be the final step in the program. Henry would meet with me and give the oral evaluation before it would be given to the President of the Congregation who flew in to attend the afternoon report. When I arrived in Henry's office at 11:00 a.m., I no sooner got seated before he proceeded to share his evaluation. He started off by saying that he felt like a school boy being reprimanded when I met with him. I said, "Henry you spent five hours testing and evaluating me and I never felt like I was a school girl being reprimanded."

For the next hour I listened in disbelief to all of his conclusions. If I had a shred of a positive self image of myself, it was totally unraveled. The final conclusion was that I had no memory and that I had impaired motor skills. I was devastated. He did make the observation that I was jovial and outgoing, which attracted others. He went on to say that I enjoyed flirting with the men. I simply listened and, when he finished, he asked if I had anything to say.

I simply said, "Henry this is your opinion of me and I can't argue with you about your opinion. That is your opinion and I just don't agree with you." With that I struggled up and left his office saying that I would see him at 1:00 p.m. with my Major Superior.

As soon as I left the office, I went to find Richard, an Anglican priest whom I had befriended. We used to meet each evening to share our day with each other. I would call him Burton and he would call me Elizabeth. He answered the knock on his door and he could see that I was stressed out. "Let's go to the chapel where we can talk in the presence of the Lord." As we sat down, I began to cry. I told him all that Henry had said about me. I was devastated. He just held my hand and said, "Jane, it's over with and now you can go on with your life. Consider the source and don't pay any heed to it." We then spent a few minutes in prayer.

My Superior was waiting for me in the foyer. She had come to receive the oral evaluation. I asked if we could go into the chapel and offer a prayer. She agreed and I could only utter a few words before the tears flowed. I prayed, "God, give me the strength and the grace to get through this second oral evaluation!" We left the chapel and proceeded to Henry's office. After introductions we sat down and Henry once again shared the oral evaluation. I saw the writing on the wall when my Superior asked if it was safe for me to live alone. Henry said, "Only if she has an advocate to make sure that she can get in and out of the bathtub and doesn't forget to turn the stove off." She than asked if it was safe for me to drive a car. "That is something you will have to find out when you go home," he responded. Undoubtedly, my Superior was happy to see that her evaluation of my living alone and driving a car matched Henry's.

As soon as the interview was over, we left for the airport. I had called Mary Jane the night before, and, amid my tears, asked if she could be at the Mother House the next morning to take me home. She said, "Jane, I will be there." I continually thank God for Mary Jane's friendship. We had a stop over in New York and thankfully I was able to get out of the bathroom stall!

We arrived in San Francisco about midnight. The Sister who accompanied me to Toronto was there to pick us up. I expressed my gratitude for all that they had done out of love and concern for me. I asked the Superior while we were waiting to be picked up if I could go home tomorrow. She said, "Jane, I don't want to discuss it." We rode to the Mother House in silence except for our companion who tried to keep up a conversation. The next morning, I got up at 6:00 a.m. and attended Mass.

I couldn't find a glass in my room and mentioned it to the Sister who managed the Mother House. She said, "Jane, I'm sure I left one in your room in the cabinet." I searched the bathroom for the cabinet. It wasn't over the sink. It was on the opposite wall. I didn't want Sister to know that I couldn't find the cabinet. It only showed how paranoid I was!

True to her word, Mary Jane knocked on my door at 9:00 a.m. I embraced her and thanked her with tears streaming down my face. "Mary Jane, I'm going home!" With that a knock came at the door and the Sister who had accompanied me to Toronto and picked us up last night, came into the room. I told her I was going home.

She said, "Not today, Jane. You are to stay until Monday when the oral evaluation will be given to the Leadership team."

"I hope you allow Mary Jane to take me home now or I will call my sister and brother-in-law and they will be here in an hour to drive me home," I said. Mary Jane pointed out that it was obvious that I was near the breaking point. She said that I needed to go home, see my doctor and get back to water therapy.

"I will take her," she said. The Sister left in anger. We arrived home at about 3:00 p.m. and I opened the door and called out to Tiger and Sweet Lady, my two cats whom I had missed dearly. They were no where to be seen. My first thought was that they had gotten out of the house. After a short time, Mary Jane said that she would take Blossom, her dog, for a walk so the cats would feel safe coming home. Sure enough, she barely got out the door and Tiger and Sweet Lady appeared. Looking back now, I must have squeezed them tightly, I was so happy to see them.

The next morning, I noticed that Mary Jane did not bring in the paper as she always does when she gets up. I asked her about it and she told me that she wanted to see if I could go out and pick up the paper. Since she brought me home without the approval of the Congregational President, she wanted to make sure that I was capable of taking care of myself. She was convinced after having spent two days and a night with me.

Three days after I arrived home, I received a registered letter from my Superior. It stated that I was to relocate to the Mother House in two weeks, or in that time frame write Rome requesting a dispensation from my vows. It was humanly impossible after living 31 years in Ukiah to move in two weeks! I had no choice but to petition Rome for a dispensation from my vows after 58 years.

18

Departure

In response to the choice of either relocating to the Mother House in two weeks, or requesting from Rome a dispensation from my vows, I chose the dispensation. I felt that I was being driven out of the Congregation after 58 years. I soon learned that when it comes to Church Authority, it is absolute. The person with the authority becomes the jury and the judge. There is no room for dialogue. In my case, authority spoke. I had no other option. I have to smile because I can hear the President say, "Jane, I did not dismiss you, you chose to leave." What choice did I have?

My doctor, Dr. Gardner, who had journeyed with me through this whole experience said, "Jane, from the beginning it was an issue of power. They couldn't reel you in so they ruled you out." It's frightening that one person has the authority to force a Sister out, after fifty-eight years in the Congregation! I felt that I was living the experience of the Inquisition when people were brought up before the tribunal and sentenced without any avenue of recourse.

A Canon lawyer was appointed to me to help me draft the letter to Rome. I received the letter in the mail from Rome granting my dispensation. The President forwarded it to me. How insensitive. I would have thought that I would be called to the Mother House and that there would be a prayer service, focusing on my departure. To add to the hurt, I received word on my answering service that, since I was no longer a member of the Congregation, I could no longer wear the habit. Since the habit consisted of the medal and ring, I was to turn them in when I went to the Mother House for the meeting with the Leadership team. Again, I thought how insensitive it was to leave a message on my answering machine asking me to return my medal and ring that I had worn for over fifty years. How much more appropriate it would have been to do this in a prayer service. Everything was so cut and cold. There was no acknowledgement of the pain I was going through, having to leave my Congregation.

On July 8, 2005, I walked up the stairs of the old Mother House and glanced down at the marble steps that I had walked up fifty eight years previously. I was accompanied by my brother-in-law, Jim. My friends, Sister Mary Jane Floyd and Sister Lucia Lodolo, were present for the meeting. I was so grateful for their presence. No one would believe what I was put through during that meeting! There was no dialogue. I was simply to listen to the financial arrangement that the Congregation was offering me. Jim held my hand through the whole ordeal. He was such a support.

The President asked me to offer the prayer. Choking back tears I prayed my Mantra, "The Lord is my refuge, the Lord is my refuge, peace and justice have met and God has set me free!" When I had finished the prayer, I felt the need to let them know my feelings. I said "You have treated me cruelly and unjust. Not one of you came to Ukiah to see if indeed it was unsafe for me to live alone or drive a car. Two of you didn't even speak to me, yet you signed a letter demanding that I relocate to the Mother House in two weeks or request a dispensation from my vows. There was no process! I pray to God that you compose a process so that no Sister will have to go through what I went through."

There was no comment. The President just repeated herself and said, "Jane, you brought this on yourself." I agreed and said that I was accepting the consequences. Jesus brought it on Himself and He was crucified.

Jim then spoke up and said, "You sent a seventy-five year old woman through three time zones, had her tested psychologically and evaluated when she was on pain medication. You took her car away. What did you expect her to do, ride a bicycle? And now you want to put her in a hole for the rest of her life. What kind of Christian women are you?"

The President then said, "Jane, do you want to tell Jim what happened or do you want me to tell him?" So much for confidentiality. I told Jim the story of how I ended up in the emergency room with an elevated blood alcohol level.

His response was, "Did she get arrested and was she brought before a judge and found guilty?"

"No," came the response.

He then said, "What is this all about?" There was no response.

Mary Jane spoke up and said, "Joan would never treat Jane this way. You have dropped a curtain down and refuse to dialogue. I don't understand you. There is no compassion or justice here."

Again there was no comment. The President went over the financial statement. Out of charity and justice, they would continue to pay me the amount of my present budget and then, in February, it would be reduced. Gratefully, they would continue to pay my rent, utilities and phone. I was assured of a roof over my head. They also included newspaper and an allotment for food.

Having gone over the paper, we rose and two of the team members recited a prayer they had prepared. The words were a blur to me as the tears flowed. How I wished that we would have had a prayer service months before. At the conclusion of the prayer, every one of the Team Members was smiling and had parting words. One said, "Remember Jane, the Mother House is always here." Another, "I want to come to Ukiah." To me, they were empty words.

We closed the elevator doors and descended to the ground floor. Sister Kathleen was there to greet us just as she was there when we arrived. She said, "I have been praying the whole time." What a friend. I walked down the tile steps, knowing that I would never walk up them again!

I can only reason that the Team, out of love for me, thought it best that I relocate to the Mother House for my own safety. Unfortunately they were operating out of an invalid psychological evaluation and no reliable information regarding my ability to live alone or drive a car. A mental health worker, Joe, who comes to Plowshares each day to be available to our guests remarked, "It's obvious that there was no process." He couldn't believe that no one visited me to see if indeed it was not safe for me to live alone. When I applied for my car insurance they deducted $130.00 from my bill because I had a perfect driving record.

A letter was sent to all of the Sisters, informing them that I was no longer a member. Almost every Sister in the Congregation expressed their support for my decision to continue my ministry to the poor and homeless in Ukiah. Several expressed that they admired me for my decision. All told me that I would always be their Sister. I could feel their love and prayers.

I wanted to let the community in Ukiah know that I chose to stay. I called Mike Geniella of the Press Democrat and told him that I had a story to tell him. We met and I explained my decision to stay in Ukiah rather than relocate to the Mother House. He was most sensitive in writing the article, informing people that I was no longer a nun. He wrote, and I quote:

> "Out of habit, she still says, "Sister Jane when answering the telephone. But after nearly six decades, activist Jane Kelly is no longer a Catholic nun. Kelly, 75, said she decided to leave her San Francisco-based Order so she could remain working in the Ukiah Valley on behalf of the poor and the homeless. 'I could not in good conscience leave my ministry here and return to the city and the security that the Order offered.'"

Mary Buckley, Executive Director of Plowshares, wrote an article in the September issue of Plowshares Advocate. I was so touched by it that it that I want to share it with you.

SHE WILL ALWAYS BE SISTER JANE TO US

Sister Jane Kelly, one of Plowshares' original founders and a longtime board member, is no longer a Catholic nun. She has decided to leave the Order of the Blessed Virgin Mary in San Francisco so that she can continue living in Ukiah. The order had requested that she move back to their Bay Area Mother House because of their concerns for her health and her living alone. Jane, however, although she remains close to the sisters in the order, says she is fine on her own, and feels it is more important to stay in Ukiah, where her work and heart have resided over three decades. Jane has always marched to the beat of her own drum, as a fierce advocate of peace, justice and caring for the poor.

Epilogue

Of all of the awards that I have received over the years, the one that I prize the most reads:

Sister Jane Kelly
Woman of Integrity Award

Sister Jane Kelly
"til I die I will not remove mine integrity from me."
Job 27:5
Woman's History Celebration
March 5, 2000
Ukiah, California

It was form this award that I took the title for my book. Hopefully, all who read my autobiography will see that I have always followed my conscience and safeguarded my integrity.

What the future holds for me is a mystery. I no longer have the sense of security which was mine when I was a member of the Sisters of the Presentation. When I could no longer remain in active ministry, I was to go to the Mother House and reside in the Care Center where I would spend my last days with my Sisters. It was the hardest sacrifice that I made to remain in Ukiah and continue my ministry to the poor and homeless. I now share their uncertain future. Such is the lot of the poor. My trust is in the Lord, and I know that he will not forsake me.

I pray daily, "The Lord is my refuge, the Lord is my refuge, peace and justice have met and God has set me free!"

978-0-595-40984-6
0-595-40984-9

Printed in the United States
113715LV00004B/314/A